WE SHOULD HANG OUT SOMETIME

WE SHOULD HANG OUT SOMETIME

EMBARRASSINGLY, A TRUE STORY

JOSH SUNDQUIST

Little, Brown and Company

New York   Boston

Also by Josh Sundquist

Just Don't Fall

AUTHOR'S NOTE: All this stuff really happened. Certain names and other identifying characteristics have been changed, and some chronology altered.

Little, Brown and Company

Hachette Book Group
1290 Avenue of the Americas, New York, NY 10104
Visit us at lb-teens.com

Little, Brown and Company is a division of Hachette Book Group, Inc. The Little, Brown name and logo are trademarks of Hachette Book Group, Inc.

The publisher is not responsible for websites (or their content) that are not owned by the publisher.

First Edition: December 2014

Library of Congress Cataloging-in-Publication Data

Sundquist, Josh.
  We should hang out sometime : embarrassingly, a true story / Josh Sundquist. — First edition.
    pages cm
  ISBN 978-0-316-25102-0 (hardcover) — ISBN 978-0-316-25101-3 (ebook) — ISBN 978-0-316-25103-7 (library edition ebook) 1. Sundquist, Josh—Juvenile literature. 2. Tumors in children—Patients—United States—Biography—Juvenile literature. 3. Ewing's sarcoma—Patients—United States—Biography—Juvenile literature. 4. Skiers with disabilities—United States—Biography—Juvenile literature. 5. Motivational speakers—United States—Biography—Juvenile literature. I. Title.
  RC281.C4S87 2014
  618.92'994—dc23

                                                                    2013041678

10 9 8 7 6 5 4 3 2 1

RRD-C

Printed in the United States of America

To true love, and to my true love.

PROLOGUE

The Not-So-Distant Past

– – ~ – – – – –

When I was twenty-five years old, it came to my attention that I had never had a girlfriend. At the time, I was actually under the impression that I was in a relationship, so as you can imagine, this bit of news came as something of a shock.

I answered the call outside on the sidewalk. You always remember exactly where you were when you found out your girlfriend has a boyfriend who isn't you.

It was my friend Dan. "Listen, no one else wanted to be the one to tell you this...."

"All right."

"I'm really sorry."

"Okay..."

"Charlotte-has-a-boyfriend." He blurted it out as one continuous word.

"Right. I mean, I know. I'm her boyfriend."

There was a pause.

"Right?" I asked.

"It's not you."

"Oh" was all I managed.

I half expected him to follow up *It's not you* with *It's me*—that being the official phrase of breakup talks—but it wasn't him, either. It was some random tool bag she met at her college.

I ended the conversation as quickly as I could. Then I stood there on the sidewalk, as if I was in one of those time-lapse shots in a movie, cars and people whizzing by on all sides of me. How could she do this to me? Why didn't she at least have the courtesy to call and tell me herself?

In retrospect, we had never actually defined the relationship. She had never actually *said* she was my girlfriend. I had just sort of, you know, assumed she was. As it turned out, my assumption was completely, totally, painfully wrong.

I had always wondered how it would feel to have a girlfriend—to know that a certain girl liked me and that I liked her, too. But every time I tried to date a girl, something would go wrong. And now there I was, twenty-five years old, and I had still never had a girlfriend.

Maybe the problem was with me, the package. Maybe girls just weren't attracted to me. Maybe I wasn't funny enough or confident enough. Or maybe it was that I looked different from everyone else.[1] Maybe girls didn't want to

---

[1] I have only five of something most people have ten of. More on this later.

be seen holding hands with me in public, didn't want to bring a person who looked like me home to meet their parents.

Something had to be wrong with me, though, even if I didn't know what it was. But I wanted to know. I had to know.

So after my call with Dan, feeling so fed up with my years of searching and failing to find a girlfriend, I decided to conduct a scientific investigation. See, I have always been pretty good at things like math and science, the realms of rational, linear analysis.

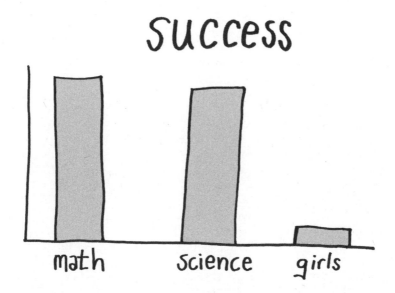

SUCCESS

math   science   girls

I figured, as I stood there on the sidewalk, that I could put my analytical skills to work on my problems with girls. I would go back in time and examine the events of my failed relationships through the lens of graphs and charts. I would then hypothesize and investigate, tracking down the girls I had tried to date and asking them, straight up: *What went wrong? Why didn't you like me? Why did you reject me?*

I would compare their answers to my hypotheses and, ultimately, draw a conclusion about the reason no one ever wanted to be my girlfriend. If it was something I could change, like an annoying habit or mannerism, I would change it. If it was some permanent physical characteristic or unalterable aspect of my personality, well, at least I would finally know the truth. And maybe the truth, as they say, would set me free.

SARAH
STEVENS

BACKGROUND

Chapter 1

— — — — — — — —

Sarah Stevens would pick truth. I knew she would.

I mean, yeah, sure, there was an outside chance she would pick dare. But since the dares on this particular day were limited by (A) the confines of a fifteen-passenger van and (B) the moral authority of its driver, there wasn't a lot of point to picking dare.

Now, generally when you play truth or dare in eighth grade, all the dares end up being some sort of expedition to explore the anatomy of the opposite gender. I dare you to put your hand here or your lips there. But not so much when you're with your church youth group, and not so much when your youth group pastor, Joe Slater, is driving, and it just so happens that he recently took the youth group to a weekend-long seminar called "I Kissed Dating Good-bye," where you learned that you should save physical exploration, including all forms of putting your hand here or your lips there, for marriage.

So in this particular church-van environment, picking dare was pointless. If you did, you would end up with something lame, gross, and improvised, like eating a left-over fast-food squeeze packet of mayonnaise or whatever.

Tony had picked truth, and then he was asked who he liked, which turned out to be some girl from his Christian school who most of us didn't know. It was kind of a letdown, but now his turn was over, and he had picked Sarah Stevens.

"Sarah, truth or dare?"

As long as she picked truth, I knew with complete certainty what he would ask her. Tony had my back.

"Truth."

Tony looked at me. We shared a slight nod. We knew what was about to go down. This was it. The Big Moment. Our chance to see if our theories were correct, if Sarah Stevens liked me the way I liked her. If she had been talking with her best friend about me the way I had been talking with Tony about her.

"Do you like Josh?" Tony asked.

Check.

Obviously, I couldn't ask her myself, even in a game of truth or dare, because that would be awkward. But I knew Tony would do it for me. I mean, he stuck with me even when I had cancer. And that's about as serious a test a friendship can face.

We had grown up two doors away from each other, Tony and me. I'd always been homeschooled and he'd always gone to Christian school, so I would spend my days waiting until he got home, when he could come outside and build forts with me.

Then: the cancer.

I was nine. I had a 50 percent chance to live. I would go to the hospital for five days, then come home for two weeks, then go back to the hospital. When I was home, I had hardly any energy. I didn't play outside. And I couldn't build forts or ride bikes or do any of the things Tony and I used to do, before I got sick, and before my left leg had to be amputated from the hip down. But you know what? Tony didn't care. He would sit inside with me and play computer games or board games or whatever it was that I had the energy to do. That long year of chemotherapy, that's when I first learned that Tony had my back.

Everyone at Covenant Presbyterian Church did, really. Even Sarah Stevens, come to think of it. She had been one of fifty kids who bought "Covenant Kids for Joshua" T-shirts. And when I first started losing my hair to the chemotherapy, Sarah's little brother, Jim, had been one of eighteen boys who gathered in my family's backyard one afternoon and shaved their heads. That's the thing about going to church. There's a bunch of extra rules you have to follow—like about dating—but the upside is that if you get cancer, if your life falls apart, church people will shave their heads and buy T-shirts for you. They will do anything they can to help you.

Sarah Stevens glanced at a couple of the girls in the van. They smiled, biting lower lips to suppress giggles. For a moment, I basked in the hope that this meant she was going to say yes.

"No," she said, looking at Tony, not at me.

I felt a hot, tingly sensation spread over my skin as I slid down a few inches against the bench seat, wishing I could just melt directly into its crusty upholstery. Not only did Sarah Stevens not like me, but she had just said so in front of all fifteen passengers in this van. It was a one-two knockout punch of rejection plus humiliation.

I disengaged from the truth or dare game until its chatter was mere background noise. After you've been shut down in front of everyone, publicly declared to be uncrushworthy by Sarah Stevens, who cares about any-

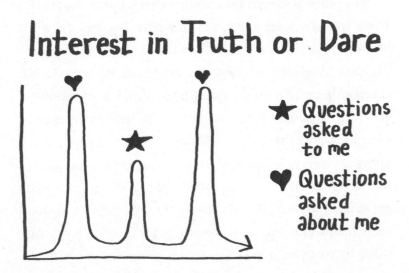

Interest in Truth or Dare

★ Questions asked to me

♥ Questions asked about me

thing else? So what if someone is gagging on a squeeze packet of mayonnaise?

At the retreat center, I set a pair of crutches on the unfinished cement floor, beneath the bunk bed I was sharing with Tony. We were staying in a rustic cabin with twenty bunk beds and a single naked lightbulb operated by a hanging string of tiny metal balls. I navigated my way through the maze of bunks to Joe Slater, who was unrolling his sleeping bag on the plastic mattress of a bottom bunk. Joe was in his late twenties, with an intense gaze, a booming laugh, and a V-shaped athletic build, all of which perfectly matched both his name (*Joe Slater!*) and his job description (*youth pastor!*).

"Hey, Joe, what are we going to do next?"

For me, not knowing the activity schedule was like living in an environment where the weather could fluctuate by one hundred degrees at any moment: I never knew what to wear.

"We're going to dinner," he said. "In the dining hall."

Dinner. Got it. Keep the prosthesis on.

Since my leg is amputated all the way up at my hip, my prosthesis includes three artificial joints: hip, knee, and ankle. Which makes the leg very heavy and cumbersome to wear.

There are a lot of amputees who run and play sports with their prostheses on. These tend to be the amputees who are popularized in the media and thus the sort who come to mind when the average person thinks of the word "amputee." But most of these amputee-athletes are below-knee amputees, meaning their legs end somewhere between the ankle and the knee. If you are a below-knee amputee, particularly if you are missing only your foot, a prosthesis can allow you to run just as fast as an able-bodied person. Above-knee amputees, though, have a harder time, because they don't have the muscles of the quadriceps to propel their knees forward. It is possible to run with an above-knee prosthesis, but it is difficult and certainly not as fast as running with a real human leg. Most difficult of all, though, is the hip-disarticulation level, which is what I am. For hip disartics, running on the prosthesis is not possible. The leg simply doesn't swing through fast enough.

So for most types of athletic activities, I would take my leg off and either run with my crutches, or set my crutches down and hop. I was faster and more agile without the leg. But I was also more self-conscious, and with the crutches, I didn't have my hands free to, say, carry a plate of food. Which is why I would wear my leg to the dining hall for dinner, and why I planned to wear it to all nonathletic social activities during the retreat.

After dinner, Joe got up and gave the rules for the weekend. The usual—no going into the other gender's cabin, no talking after lights-out, no going off anywhere by yourself. Stuff like that. Then Joe told us to open our Bibles, and he gave a "talk," which is youth-group-speak for a sermon. The usual—no getting distracted by worldly pursuits, no motives except to bring glory to God, no sexual or impure thoughts. Stuff like that.

He prayed and then announced that we were all meeting by the lake in ten minutes. Prosthesis still on, I walked over to Joe.

"What are we going to do next?" I asked.

Joe frowned, not wanting to ruin the surprise.

"By the lake?" I persisted.

"Don't tell anyone...but it's nighttime capture the flag."

"Cool, thanks."

That meant leg off, using crutches, so I would be able to run. Of course, even with my crutches, I wasn't an especially useful teammate in capture the flag—I couldn't really hold the flag and move at the same time. But at least on the crutches I could run around to make it look like I was participating. The participation would be fake, but what did that matter when the alternative was wearing, you know, a fake leg? That's what it means to be an amputee: You're always putting on a show.

Down by the lake, we divided into teams, counting off by ones and twos. I tried to shift in line so I could be on the same team as Sarah Stevens. It worked. Not that I was going to talk to her or anything, not after her bombshell during truth or dare, but for some reason it seemed important that we be on the same team, working together to capture the same flag.

Chapter 2

— – ~ — — — — — —

On Saturday morning, after a pancake breakfast, I did not have to ask Joe what we were going to do next because he announced it to the group: hiking at Shenandoah National Park. It was going to be an all-day trip, and we should wear our bathing suits under our hiking clothes.

When we loaded into vans for the drive to the hiking trail, something totally insane happened: Sarah Stevens sat beside me. We were so close that one of her two legs and my one leg were—almost—touching. And it's not like she *had* to sit beside me. There had been other vans. There had been other rows with available seats in this van. She *chose* to sit beside me. Which made me wonder—what if she liked me after all? Maybe she was lying yesterday in truth or dare?

I thought about this as I walked along the hiking trail. It really did seem like she liked me. Not only had she sat beside me in the van, but sometimes when I looked at her, like this morning at breakfast or last night during Joe's talk, she was *already looking at me* and then we would both look away from each other.

The trail eventually led to a waterfall. It was a for-real one, too, like what you'd see on a postcard, about one hundred feet of vertical drop. While the rest of the group was splashing around in the foamy pool underneath, I climbed by myself up a trail so steep you had to grab on to exposed tree roots to keep from slipping. It was tricky because I'd have to let go of my forearm crutch handle for a second, allowing the cuff of the crutch to dangle from my wrist, while I grabbed at the root and pulled myself up like on a chin-up bar. At the top, there was a rock the size of a small car that jutted out over the falls. Sitting on it was a guy and a girl, midtwenties, with their arms draped over each other's shoulders, sharing what appeared to be some kind of homemade cigarette.

"Hey, kid," the guy said to me.

"Hey," I said.

"This place is legit, huh?"

"Very legitimate, yes."

"How old are you?"

"Thirteen."

"You got a girlfriend?"

I thought about Sarah Stevens.

"No."

The guy took a drag on the cigarette.

"Let me give you a tip. Once you get yourself a girlfriend," he said, nodding his chin toward the girl he was intertwined with, "bring her right here. Sit on this rock."

He winked at me as if I should understand. I didn't, but nodded anyway.

"Trust me," he said. "You'll be glad you did."

"Cool. Thanks."

When we got back to the retreat center that afternoon, I found Joe Slater.

"What are we gonna do next?" I said.

"Showers. Then dinner."

"What about after that?"

Joe looked away for a second, squinting into the woods.

"Listen, Josh, sometimes it's best to just go with the flow. To have some faith that God will take care of things. Every moment of your life doesn't need to be planned out in advance. Sometimes the best moments are the spontaneous ones you don't plan for. You get what I'm saying?"

His words were true in the way most things printed on greeting cards are true. But I wasn't asking him about the schedule because I had a problem with spontaneity. I was asking because I needed to know whether or not to wear my leg. Only, I didn't want to tell Joe, because doing so would violate my Rules of Being an Amputee.

I had developed these rules during the three years since I'd lost my leg. It wasn't like I sat down one day and said, "What are some good rules I can write for myself?"

Instead, they had taken root and sprouted without conscious attention, like weeds in my mind. And they grew in the exact opposite direction of how it feels to be an amputee. They were a correction—or maybe an overcorrection.

These were my rules:

1. Never be a burden.
2. Never be different.

As Joe and I stood there by the vans in the gravel parking area, wearing T-shirts and semiwet bathing suits, towels draped over our shoulders, I considered telling him the reason I always wanted to know the schedule: I needed to decide whether to wear my leg or not. But doing so would violate both of my rules. It would make me a burden, because if he knew I was making a decision about whether or not to wear a prosthesis based on each activity he planned, it might affect the way he planned the schedule. Instead of thinking, Would this be a fun activity for the students? he'd be thinking, I wonder if Josh will want to wear his prosthesis for this game? Or maybe he will already be on his crutches at this point in the day, which would mean we should play this other game instead. And obviously, telling him would violate rule number two as well, because it would identify me as different. I mean, no one else in the youth group was fluctuating their limb count depending on the activity.

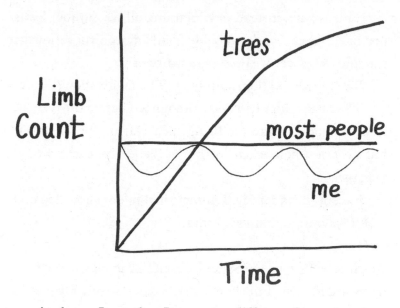

And yes, I get that I *was* very different from everyone else. I was visually different, conspicuously different, obviously different. All you had to do was look at me. I was missing a leg. Either I was using crutches and there was no leg there at all or I was wearing one that didn't look quite right and caused me to limp.

So yeah, I was different, and there was nothing I could do about it. But when you're faced with a significantly life-altering negative situation you can't control, you grasp at the little things you *can* control. The little opportunities where you can make choices for yourself. I couldn't choose to get my leg back, no, but I could choose to ask my youth pastor about the schedule without telling him my hip-disarticulated leg was the reason I was asking.

This is why, instead of explaining all this to Joe, I was just like, "Yeah, that's probably good advice. But seriously, though: What are we doing after dinner?"

Joe sighed and then smirked. "The talent show."

The talent show had been announced before the retreat, in case people wanted to bring their clarinet or whatever, but no one knew when in the weekend the event would take place.

Except, now, for me. Dinner, then talent show: leg on.

"Okay, cool, thanks," I said.

At the talent show, Joe Slater himself had an act, one where he awarded "Most likely to"–style superlatives. He would say someone's name and then make a reference to something funny that had happened at the retreat, like *Most likely to walk into a spiderweb on the hike* or *Most likely to snore*, and then everyone would laugh and cheer.

"Josh Sundquist," he read off his list. "Most likely to ask, 'What are we going to do next?' "

He impersonated me using an annoying little kid's voice. I felt a stab of betrayal, like Joe had revealed a secret I'd confided in him. But it was my fault. I had chosen not to tell him why. I was confident he would have happily given me the entire schedule printed on a sheet of paper a week in advance of the retreat, if that's what I wanted. And if he had known, certainly he would not have made a joke about it in the talent show. People will bend over backward to be helpful and accommodating if they know it's about your disability.

But I had chosen to keep the reason a secret *because* it was about my disability. Because I didn't want to be a burden. Because I didn't want to be different. And ironically, this had led to both of my rules being broken. Even though I never told him why I was asking, I had clearly become a burden to Joe. Otherwise he wouldn't have given me the "award." That was the joke here: I had asked so many times that I had become annoying. And a burden. And because none of the other students had overheard me asking Joe for the frequent schedule updates, no one actually got the joke, so they didn't laugh at my award like they did the others. My award was met with awkward silence, and then a smattering of applause. Which made me feel very different indeed.

I stole a peek at Sarah Stevens. She was staring at me. When our eyes met, she looked away.

Chapter 3

— — — — — — — —

As far as periods of life go, middle school gets a lot of hate. But there's one really, really good thing about middle school, which is that if someone likes you, there is a 100 percent chance that you are going to find out, because he or she will tell someone who will in turn tell someone else, and after five more minutes everyone within a fifty-mile radius, including you, will know about it. And fortunately, gossip travels just as well through the social fabric of a church youth group as it does through a school.

As it happens, I found out that Sarah Stevens liked me through instant message. I was talking to Tony, who had heard it via instant message through Sarah's best friend, Eileen Adair. So the information was very close to the source. In fact, it had never progressed beyond the level of best friends, so it was pretty much guaranteed to be true.

I replied to Tony with an excessive amount of unnecessary punctuation, like, **ARE YOU SERIOUS!?!!!???!?!!????**

Tony was indeed serious, and furthermore, it turned out Sarah Stevens was pretty serious, too—at least serious enough that she wanted to go out with me. Yes. You read that correctly. *Sarah Stevens wanted to go out with me.* This bit of information, also revealed via Tony, boggled my mind. I stared at the computer screen in disbelief, my face alternating between slack-jawed shock and wide-mouthed grin.

Sarah Stevens liked me! She liked me after all! She had lied in truth or dare—I was the one she liked!

But as amazing as it was, none of it mattered. Because I wasn't allowed to date until I was sixteen years old.

Mom and Dad had always had that rule, since I was little. No dating until you're sixteen. So from the beginning, my interest in Sarah and whether or not she liked me back had been a purely hypothetical exercise. But what if...what if...they would make an exception for Sarah Stevens?

Conservative is the very best description of my parents, for that is what they are in every sense of the word. Not just politically and religiously (although that, too), but also environmentally (we always had a rotting compost pile of peels and skins and other food scraps in the backyard, which Mom used as fertilizer for her vegetable garden) and economically. Especially economically. For example, let's say there's a mouse living in the kitchen. My mom will set out one of those little disposable wooden mousetraps with a piece of food on it and catch the mouse. But rather than throw the whole mess away, like most people would, my mom removes by hand the bloodied, partially decapitated rodent carcass and then cleans, disinfects, and resets the mousetrap so she can reuse it, rather than throw away the first one with its dangling mouse appendages and spend a dollar—*a dollar*—to buy a new one.

Both my parents are wire-frame skinny, my mom because she's a raw vegan, and my dad because he's married to one. As men grow old, the waistline of their pants tends to sink down beneath an expanding gut, or if they stay thin, their pants creep up on their chest. I'm confident my dad will fall into the second group, eventually turning torso-less, just a gray-haired head and bean-pole arms popping out of a pair of wool trousers hiked up to his armpits like a strapless dress.

But I digress. The point is that as extremely conservative people, my parents want everything to stay the same. Or, even better, to return to the way things used to be. So, as I learned at a young age, if you need to persuade them of something, one technique is to frame your argument around the idea that you are making a case for these values.

I made my opening statement the next Sunday while we were driving home from church in our minivan. Mom and Dad were up front. My nine-year-old brother, Matthew, was beside me in the way back, and in the middle sat my five-year-old brother, Luke, and a car seat containing our newly arrived baby sister, Anna.

"So you know how we've always been friends with the Stevens family?" I asked my parents.

I paused to allow them to mentally confirm that yes,

we had indeed always been friends with the Stevenses. In fact, Mom and Dad would no doubt be remembering that the Stevenses had been in our homeschool group for a year when Mrs. Stevens homeschooled Sarah. And as I said before, Sarah's brother Jim had shaved his head for me when I had cancer. Now he and I were in the same Boy Scout troop. Dad and Mr. Stevens were tennis partners. So obviously this was how things had always been.

"Yeah..." said Dad, in a tone that said, *I know you're trying to set us up here, I just haven't figured out how yet.*

"Well, I thought of a great idea to ensure that our families remain close," I said in my best "mature young man" voice.

"What's that?" asked Dad.

"I should go out with Sarah."

"Go out with her where?" asked Mom.

"We wouldn't go anywhere," I said. "I mean, we would just be boyfriend-girlfriend."

"You mean like go steady?" asked Dad.

"I don't know what that means," I answered.

"It's when you stop dating multiple people and date just one girl," said Dad.

"Why would you be dating multiple people at the same time?" I asked.

"You know, like maybe you take Betty-Sue out on Friday and take Barbara out on Saturday, and then you decide you want to only go out with Barbara," he said.

"So you're cheating on Betty-Sue?"

"No—no, I said..." Dad stammered.

"Then you're cheating on Barbara?"

"No, you're dating both of them."

"At the same time? Do they know about each other?" I asked, confused.

"Yes. No. I mean, maybe they do. It doesn't matter. Not unless you're going steady with one of them, which means you aren't dating anyone else."

"Okay, well, people don't do that anymore," I said. "Now you only go out with one person. No one dates more than one person at the same time."

"Hmm," said Dad.

It was not lost on me that the subject had been changed. "So anyways, can I date Sarah?"

"We'll have to think about it," said Mom, her go-to phrase for a soft, kindhearted no.

"All right, well, just so you know, she likes me and wants to go out with me, so if I'm not allowed to go out with her, that might make our friendship with the Stevens family kind of awkward," I said.

The friendship we've always had, I could've added, but by the way Mom and Dad glanced worriedly at each other, I could tell I'd already scored a direct hit on their conservative fears.

In the coming weeks, additional rules and boundaries were set up "for my protection." No touching, other than hugging, which had to be brief, no lingering. No seeing her without adult supervision. Not more than twenty minutes on the phone per day. Yeah, fine, whatever. I agreed to each of their stipulations with all the thought and care I put into reading an update to the iTunes User Agreement Terms and Conditions.

It was a big night, one of the biggest of my life, so I chose my very coolest clothes. I wore my light blue suede skater shoes, both of them, one on each foot, because I was wearing my leg. Over the top of said prosthesis I chose my cool jeans: dark wash with a wide, straight cut. I'd bought them at T.J.Maxx for thirty-six dollars, a purchase that had required not buying any other clothes for three and a half months in order to save up — because my parents gave me a thrift-store-sized clothing budget of only ten dollars per month to buy all my clothes.[2] A subcommittee composed of Eileen and Tony had arranged for this to be the night. Furthermore, the subcommittee had agreed that Sarah would say yes in response to my question. Even so, I was insanely nervous as I walked up to her before youth group started.

Signaling that she had been waiting for this moment and wanted it to be semiprivate, Sarah took a few steps away from her group of friends, meeting me halfway across

---

[2] Whenever I argued this was not enough money to fill a wardrobe, my parents would respond that if I bought everything at the Salvation Army Thrift Store on its monthly ninety-nine-cent day, I could buy ten new (well, new to me) items per month.

the room. She was wearing her bright red ski jacket and a big smile. I felt the effects of adrenaline as I walked toward her, real leg, fake leg, real leg, fake leg: the tightness in my chest, the constricted blood vessels, my pulsing heart pumping blood into my flushed cheeks.

"Hi," I said. We did not hug. In fact, we remained well out of each other's personal space, like strangers talking on the sidewalk at a bus stop.

"Hi," she said, still smiling.

"Will you go out with me?" I had rehearsed the words enough times that they tumbled out on top of each other in one simultaneous burst. Fortunately, since she had been expecting the question, Sarah was able to decipher my meaning.

Her smile broadened, if that was even possible. "Yes!"

I nodded a few times in thoughtful approval. "Cool."

I gave her a high five, like a handshake sealing a gentle-man's agreement. And then I walked away.

I want to be clear, though: There was a lot of thinking in between those two sentences, in between the high-fiving and the walking away.

I thought: Nice! Cool! We're going out. So...now what? What am I supposed to do now? Hold her hand? Talk to her? But what would we talk about? What do girls like to talk about? Makeup? Glitter? I didn't really know. I had never thought about this part. I had always thought about whether she liked me, and whether she would say yes if I asked her out. Never about what would happen if we were actually going out.

Ergo, I walked away. Fled the scene. Hit and run.

I found Tony. He raised his eyebrows expectantly.

"She said yes!"

He gave me a high five.

But when youth group started a few minutes later, Sarah had disappeared. Just vanished.

Part of me was sad. I had wanted to sit near her, or maybe even *in the chair right beside hers*, during the talk. Let other people wonder if we might be going out. That sort of thing. But a bigger part of me felt wonderfully, gloriously relieved. With Sarah gone, I didn't have to worry about talking to her or holding her hand or wondering how I was supposed to behave now that we were going out. It was a lot of pressure, this going-out business, and not having to actually interact with my new girlfriend definitely made the having-a-girlfriend part way easier.

The next day, while I was doing my schoolwork at my desk in my room, I thought about Sarah, how she was at school with her friends. I wondered if maybe she was thinking about me, especially now that we were going out. I wondered if she was bragging to her friends, *Josh Sundquist asked me out last night! We are totally going out now!* I hoped so.

That afternoon, I went online and waited for Sarah to sign in. Finally, late in the afternoon, an instant message

How Much I Talked to Sarah Stevens

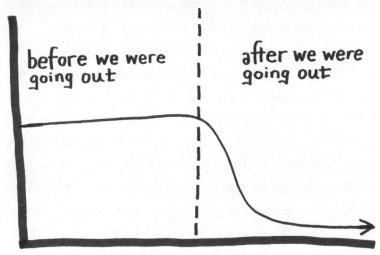

before we were going out

after we were going out

popped up on my screen. But it wasn't from Sarah. It was from her BFF, Eileen.

hi, sarah just wants to be friends, the message said.

It knocked the wind out of me. I didn't know what to say in response. Finally, I typed:

Me: **are you breaking up with me?**

Sarah's BFF: **well sarah is. but she still wants to be friends.**

Me: **why?**

Sarah's BFF: **because she values your friendship**

Me: **no i mean why is she breaking up with me?**

Sarah's BFF: **she thinks going out will hurt your friendship.**

Me: **ok thanks for telling me.**

I signed off and went into my room and shut the door and cried into my pillow. My first relationship. Ended after twenty-three hours, almost before it even began. I was angry and confused and sad. Why hadn't she told me herself? Why did she have her friend tell me? And why over instant message? She could've at least had the decency to ask her friend to break up with me in person, or through a carefully worded handwritten letter on embossed stationery. An instant message just seemed so casual, so cheap, like our relationship was a crumb Sarah was wiping off the table with a flick of the back of her hand. She still wanted to be friends? Really?

A few weeks later, I deleted my instant messenger account. I was done with chatting online. It was too easy to be someone you're not, to say things you wouldn't otherwise. Like how you liked someone, or how you wanted to break up with them. If you weren't willing to say it to me in person, I didn't want to hear it from you online.

After those twenty-three hours, our families weren't as close as we used to be. Things changed after all. Oops. Sorry, Mom and Dad. And so I was left alone with my questions: Why didn't Sarah give me a chance to prove myself as a boyfriend? And where had she disappeared to at youth group after I asked her out?

HYPOTHESIS

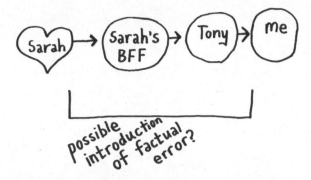

Subject behavior — breaking up with me approximately twenty-three hours after the initial onset of our romantic relationship — suggests that she may not have had romantic feelings toward me to begin with. This would indicate a possible error in the chain of gossip that had led me to believe such feelings existed.[3]

Interview with subject is required to validate hypothesis.

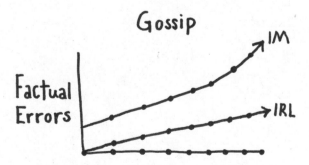

---

[3] Anecdotal evidence does suggest that factual errors may be created when information is passed between BFFs, particularly if said information is shared via online chatting platforms. In fact, there is a direct correlation between the number of times a piece of information has been passed along and the number of factual errors it contains.

INVESTIGATION

Chapter 4

I arrived before Sarah Stevens. It had been more than ten years since Sarah and I "went out" for twenty-three hours. I didn't count her as my first girlfriend. If I did, she would be my only girlfriend, and having had one twenty-three-hour girlfriend is much sadder than having had no girlfriends at all. So that's what I told myself: I've never had a girlfriend. If it doesn't last at least one day, it doesn't count.

That said, Sarah Stevens was still a significant blip on my romantic radar, and all these years I'd been curious to understand why she broke up with me so fast. So there I was.

It was a few days before Christmas. I looked out the windows of Starbucks and saw the snow on the sidewalk. It would be a white Christmas, something you don't see very often in Harrisonburg, Virginia. Sarah and I were both in town visiting our families for the holidays. I had sent her a message on Facebook a few days before about getting coffee.

She arrived late, following a string of apologetic text messages about not having a car, her dad having to drive her, and his driving very slowly in the snow. She walked in wearing a beret that suggested—accurately—that she was now an actor living in New York. We hugged (no lingering, of course), ordered drinks, and sat down by the window. We caught up on the facts: She just got cast for a production of *Les Misérables*. What part? Cosette, one of the leads. What was her living situation? Looking for a new roommate on Craigslist. How was it being back home? Reminds her how much nicer people are here in Harrisonburg than in New York. That sort of thing. It was easy to like her and to see why I *like*-liked her back when I was thirteen.

I couldn't really think of a particularly smooth segue, so I began with, "It's weird to think we were...you know... sort of like together for a little while there in middle school."

She laughed. I noticed she had this two-syllable chuckle that was always perched just beneath the surface, ready to jump out at the slightest sign of humor. *Hee-HUH.*

She said, "Actually, since I was going to see you today, I went through my old diaries at my parents' house. I found some stuff about you!"

I had to resist the urge to jump across the table and grab her shoulders and scream, *What? I'm in your diary? You read it this morning? Tellmetellmetellme!*

Instead, I responded with deliberate restraint, one eyebrow cocked in casual curiosity. Interested but not desperate. "Stuff about me, you say?"

"Yeah, like one time we were going to this retreat together, I wrote about it...."

My mind: retreat? Retreat! You wrote about the retreat? TELLMETELLMETELLME!

My mouth: silent. Nodding.

"Anyway, we were in the van, and I guess we were playing truth or dare or something...."

The truth or dare game!

"And someone asked if I liked you, but you were sitting right there, so I lied...."

What? It was a *lie*?

"And I said that I didn't like you even though I totally had a huge crush on you."

With this she burst out laughing, overcome by the humor of this story from her diary. I laughed, too. I mean, what else was I going to do? How do you react to that? When it turns out that Sarah definitely liked you after all, that she admits to lying in truth or dare?

"Wow, that's...uh...hilarious," I said. "I remember that retreat." Oh yes. I remember.

"That was such a long time ago," she said.

I take a sip of my green tea. "Yeah. Remember how we dated for, like, a day?"

She burst out laughing again—not her two-syllable giggle but an all-out laugh, as if I had just hit the punch line of a killer joke.

"I remember." She paused, some more laughs bubbling up. "I mainly remember when you asked me out, I think it was at youth group or something, and you were like, 'Will you go out with me?' and I was like, 'Yeah,' and then you were like, 'Cool,' and then you just"—here she laughed some more, the memory obviously reaching its crescendo—"walked away. And I was so freaked out. I'd never had a boyfriend before. I was like, Oh my gosh, Josh is never going to talk to me again! Now that we are going out, we aren't going to be friends anymore!"

"I remember you, like, disappeared right after I asked you out."

"Oh yeah, I asked one of the leaders, I think it was Melissa..." She struggled for the last name.

"Bruning?" I offered.

"Yeah, Melissa Bruning came with me to the bathroom, and I just cried the whole rest of the night, and she talked me through it," Sarah said. She was still smiling, amused by the story even though we were talking about a time when she, it turns out, was crying. Yes, crying. Because I asked her out. That's a bad sign for your dating life right there, if girls burst out crying when you ask them out.

"So you were worried we wouldn't be friends anymore?"

"Well, yeah," she said. "I mean, you literally walked away immediately after asking me out. It was sooo awkward. I figured we probably wouldn't talk at all if we were boyfriend and girlfriend."

"You were probably right," I admitted.

"So when you walked away like that, I could see that our friendship would be ruined if we dated, so I just—I just—" She seemed to struggle with the words to describe our breakup, as if she was having to dump me right now all over again and wished she could call on a BFF to come to her rescue. "I don't know—"

I threw her a line. "No, that makes sense," I said. "I was pretty awkward."

And as I said it, I thought: Probably I still am, judging by the number of girlfriends I've had.

"We both were," she said.

I didn't recall her ever being awkward, but that's the funny thing about awkwardness: You can never tell how much of it is in your head and how much of it is real. Because if you ask the other person if it's real—that is, if she feels it, too—then automatically it is. Because discussing awkwardness is always, well, awkward.

LIZA TAYLOR
SMITH

BACKGROUND

Chapter 5

Of all the socially awkward behaviors I exhibited during my transition from homeschool to public school in ninth grade, perhaps the most outrageous was my decision to memorize everyone in the eighth-grade yearbook so I could greet all my classmates by name on the first day of school. And of all those faces I memorized, perhaps the one I was most looking forward to acquainting myself with in real life was that of Liza Taylor Smith.

In her yearbook photo, she had seductively droopy eyelids that reminded me of old photos I'd seen of Marilyn Monroe. These eyes were counterbalanced by a friendly smile. The smile was warm enough to suggest that, despite her beauty, she would be kind to any member of the male species who might show an interest in her, including even dorky former homeschoolers with one leg.

Liza Taylor Smith. I loved how, unlike everyone else, she had not two but three words in her name, as if her hotness could not be described by or contained within the confines of a normal name structure. Was Taylor a second first name? If so, why wasn't it hyphenated, like Liza-Taylor? So many questions! We would obviously have a lot to talk about when we finally met on the first day of school.

When people think of homeschooling, they often picture a child sitting at a desk in the kitchen, the mother teaching multiplication tables by scribbling numbers on a blackboard magnetized to the refrigerator. There are plenty of approaches to homeschooling, and people homeschool for many different reasons, but ours functioned less like a one-student classroom and more like an independent study.

At the start of the school year, Mom would give me my

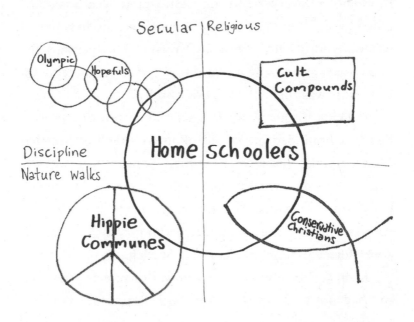

textbooks, one for each subject. She would divide the number of pages by the number of days in the school year, and those would be my daily reading requirements. That was basically it. So I learned to be self-motivated. In elementary school, I would get up at 7 AM and not come out of my room for breakfast until I was finished with all my schoolwork for the day. That's why, when I was approaching my first day of public school, my natural inclination was to borrow a yearbook from one of my friends at church and start memorizing the facts. Because that's what I knew how to do. It had always been my approach to school. Read. Memorize. Repeat.

Back in elementary school, during the finish-all-the-work-before-breakfast days, homeschooling seemed so much better than traditional school. By the time Tony got home at four in the afternoon, I'd already been building forts in the bushes for six hours. Then I hit middle school, and my friends in the neighborhood started telling me about the glorious adventures they were having at public school: PE class. Dances. Pretty girls. Everywhere. Suddenly homeschooling didn't seem so fun anymore.

Mom and Dad weren't so excited about the idea. Christian school, maybe. But public school? It was a well-known fact among Christian homeschoolers that public schools were bastions of gangs, drugs, teen pregnancy, rap music, pop culture, secular humanism, witchcraft, and body piercings.

Mom, Dad, and I would sit around our smooth, laminate kitchen table after dinner, arguing about whether I should be allowed to attend public school starting in ninth grade.

"Joshua, if you go to public school…" Dad lowered his voice in case Matthew or Luke was listening from the family room. "Your English teacher might ask you to read *pornographic* novels."

I was very curious to know what exactly a pornographic novel was, but decided it was better not to ask.

"And you'll probably be invited to join a gang," he added.

"In your first week," said Mom.

"Don't worry," I said. "I'll be sure to wait until offers come in from all the gangs before I make my final decision."

Mom's face dropped.

"I'm kidding!" I said. "Look, I'm not going to join a gang. Obviously."

"They will peer-pressure you," said Mom.

This I did not doubt. Nor did I doubt that there were gangs, or that I would be asked to join one. These were facts that homeschoolers like me took for granted. The pope is Catholic. Bears poop in the woods. Public school kids are in gangs that deal drugs.

But to me, the benefits outweighed those risks.

"I can resist peer pressure. But in homeschool I don't

have the opportunities I would at regular school. I really think God wants me there."

Also: *I* wanted to go to public school. I wanted to be on the newspaper staff, to attend school dances, to meet hundreds of pretty girls. But for my parents, what God wanted was more important than what I wanted. And God was more difficult to argue with, since he wasn't sitting at the table with us. So I played the God card whenever I could.

"We'll pray more about it," said Dad.

Eventually, and after much more prayer, Dad joined my and God's side, and Mom was outvoted.

Having been indoctrinated my entire life about the dangers of public school, I walked through the heavy doors on my first day feeling how I imagine an American spy would feel upon entering a terrorist training camp for four years of deep-undercover work. I had a panicky fear in my chest that was screaming, *You do not belong here! You are going to say the wrong thing! Your whole cover will be blown!*

Before first period, I glanced quickly in the locker below mine as a student opened it. He was a few grades older than me, so I didn't feel confident saying hi to him, but he lived in my neighborhood and I knew who he was. Anyway, I looked into his locker for the sole purpose of finding out which area he was using to stash his drugs and weapons. Not to determine *whether* he had drugs and weapons, mind you, but merely to determine where they were, because there was absolutely no doubt in my mind that he, like most students at public school, hid both drugs and weapons in his locker.

Though I was intimidated, I had made up my mind that I would try to befriend as many of my fellow freshmen as possible. And it would be easy since I already knew who they were. As I walked down the hall, I called out their names and waved at students I recognized from the yearbook. I'd spent so long looking at their photos that they had become like celebrities to me. The school hallway was like a red carpet before the Academy Awards. I shouted first and last names with glee, waving frantically, getting that OMG-a-celebrity-just-waved-back-at-me rush whenever my greeting was returned. I scanned the halls most earnestly for that one particular face, that perfect face with the droopy eyelids and inviting smile, the face of Liza Taylor Smith. But I didn't see her en route to first period.

As I said, it felt like I was going undercover. Not only because I was new to public school but also because I was an amputee wearing a prosthesis, a device that is made to look like something other than what it really is. There is a deception there, and as with all deception, the implicit mission is to keep the secret, to not let anyone find out. I wore long, long shorts — so long you might think they were pants — exposing just a few inches of ankle in between my shoe and the shorts. My artificial leg was covered in foam molded to the shape of my real leg, and that foam was covered in a rubber "skin" matched to my real skin tone. I wasn't too far along in puberty yet, so there wasn't enough hair on my right leg to make the shins look mismatched. To the casual onlooker who passed me in the hall, I reminded myself with every step, my leg would look real. No one could tell. No one would know. My secret was safe.

Yet despite my very best efforts to walk smoothly, when you have an artificial hip, knee, and ankle joint on one side, you're always going to have at least a slight limp. An upperclassman stuck out his leg in front of my feet as I walked by him on my way to lunch. I tripped, letting my books fly as I put out my arms to break my fall.

His friends laughed.

"You ain't no pimp! So don't try and walk like one!" he yelled, exchanging celebratory high fives with his entourage.

I lifted myself up to a push-up position and rolled my weight onto my real foot so my prosthetic knee straightened out behind me. Then I brought my real foot between my hands so I was positioned like a sprinter before a race. Pressing from the muscles in my real leg—my fake one of course provided no assistance in these situations—I stood up. Not to face him. I didn't look back. I kept my eyes on the ground, bending over to pick up my books, feeling my lower lip quiver.

I made a quick glance around the hallway. Had Liza Taylor Smith seen this? That would be just my luck. But no, fortunately, she was not around. She did not see me fall. This incident would remain a secret from her. As for the people who had seen it happen, there was no way to tell if they had figured out I had a prosthesis. I put my head back down and kept walking.

Later that first day I had Honors Biology class, where the teacher, Mr. Glick, taught us about the nine phyla of the animal kingdom. As he spoke, I saw other students jotting down the names of the phyla in their notebooks, but I had never had to listen to someone and write down what they were saying (*at the same time!*) before. I had always learned from reading books in my bedroom. So I didn't take any notes.

On the second day of Honors Biology, Mr. Glick said, "Take out a sheet of paper for…" He literally paused for dramatic effect. "Our pop quiz."

Around the room, there were several audible gasps. Three-ring binders were snapped open to slide out notebook paper; at other desks, sheets of paper were torn out of spiral-bound notebooks with a *zzzzzzip*. I clicked open my own three-ring binder and pulled out a sheet, the paper shaking in my hand as I set it on my desk. I was thinking: a "pop quiz"? What is this? What's going on? Why didn't he tell us about it ahead of time?

"Please close your notebooks and textbooks. At the top of your paper write your name."

I wrote my name slowly, doing my best to keep my pen from shaking.

Writing My Name

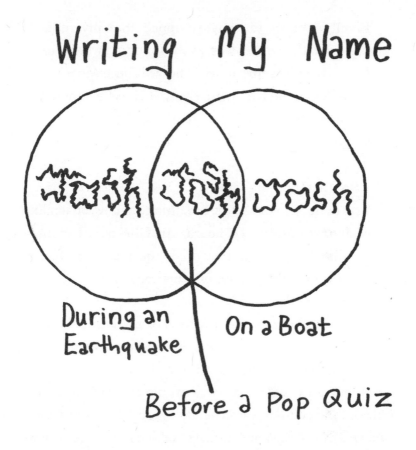

During an Earthquake

On a Boat

Before a Pop Quiz

"Now write down the nine phyla in the animal kingdom."

I was screwed.

I had not taken any notes. I had not listened carefully. I had not known it was important or, for that matter, even known how to learn that way. It was so unfair! A pop quiz...with no advance warning! Public school was a rip-off! I was going to fail out and not get into college and end up destitute and living on the streets.

Finally, one of the phyla popped into my mind. I remembered it because it was a cool-sounding word: "nematode." I thought some more, and two additional words from the lesson added themselves, shakily, to my handwritten list:

Arthropod.

Mollusk.

After that: nothing.

I sat there, pen unsteady, breathing shallow, struggling to recall anything else I'd heard Mr. Glick say. I thought about animals I'd seen at the zoo, at the aquarium. I knew plenty of animal names, but not their phyla.

"Pencils down, please."

And just like that, the quiz was over. With only three out of nine answers on my paper, my best possible score was a 33 percent. My life was headed for ruin.

A few weeks later, Mr. Glick would reveal that the pop quiz did not count toward the final grade. It was just a lesson, he said, on the importance of taking notes and reviewing them before class. Well, Mr. Glick, lesson learned. I started taking notes after that quiz. Never again did I score so low on a quiz or test.

But the most significant event for me romantically on that first day was what *didn't* happen: I did not meet Liza Taylor Smith.

Chapter 6

After school let out, I was talking to two guys I knew from the yearbook, Ryan Eckhart and Craig Johansson, while also looking around for Liza Taylor Smith. Was she out here on the sidewalk anywhere? Maybe she had gotten a haircut. Maybe she didn't look like she did in her yearbook photo, and that's why I hadn't recognized her.

"Question," I said to Ryan. "One person I haven't met yet is Liza Taylor Smith. You know her?"

"Liza Taylor? Of course. Hottest girl in our class."

I nodded. "So...is she nearby anywhere? Do you see her?"

Ryan searched the groups of students. "Uhhhh...no, she's not here."

"Bummer. I really want to meet her."

"Yeah? Just watch for a big group of guys who are all trying to talk to her. She'll be right in the middle."

Craig added, "Or look for the girl with really big, you

know." He cupped his hands in front of his chest, and I realized that he was talking about...Liza Taylor Smith's breasts! I was shocked. I had never, ever discussed any girl's breasts before. To hear this guy talk about, well, *female anatomy* so openly, without even lowering his voice, as if he didn't care if anyone overheard him, made me tense up uncomfortably.

I left Ryan and Craig and talked with a few other groups of students, mostly girls, none of whom included Liza Taylor Smith or her apparently noteworthy breasts. Finally, Mom pulled up to the curb. Later, at dinner, when I told her about the kid who had tripped me, she started crying. Public school was everything she had been afraid it would be.

After a week had passed and I still had not been offered drugs or gang membership, nor had I seen a single weapon fall out of a locker or a backpack, I started to wonder if maybe homeschoolers were wrong about some aspects of public school. Because actually, most of the students I'd met had been pretty nice. Public school students were, for the most part, nice people who were very similar to me, other than the fact that they had two legs and talked about girls' breasts.

That was the good news. The bad news was that I still had not crossed paths with Liza Taylor Smith. I realized we must have had different walking routes between classes.

Which wasn't that surprising. Our school was an enormous web of interconnected wings, hallways, and stairwells that crisscrossed like highway overpasses. So I started varying my routes between my locker and class, trying to increase the likelihood I would bump into her. And whenever I was in a crowd, like at lunch or outside after school, I would ask around to see if anyone had seen Liza Taylor Smith nearby.

After two weeks of this, I had pretty much given up hope that we would ever meet. That's when I received the Letter.

It was handed to me by Lauren Baker, a well-known member of Liza Taylor Smith's entourage, who happened to sit beside me in Spanish. Lauren was a pretty, aloof girl who generally deemed me worthy of only a slight smile and nod when I said hi to her.

That was one thing I had learned about public school. It was a place with *places*: a well-defined social hierarchy in which everyone knew his or her status. That was weird to me—I'd been taught not to buy into stereotypes, because stereotypes are shallow and untrue and everything. But all the high school stereotypes you hear about in popular culture seemed to be true at Harrisonburg High School: The quarterback of the football team dated the cheerleading captain. Guys with sports cars had hot girlfriends. The really, really smart students wore glasses and had acne.

As this picture of social structure had become clearer

in my mind, my fantasies about hitting it off with Liza Taylor Smith had grown dimmer. From what I could tell, she sat atop the very pinnacle of popularity in our grade. She was a cheerleader. She was hot. She had certain characteristics the other guys liked to talk about. Need I say more?

Me, well, I didn't really know where I fit in. I didn't have an established clique of friends like everyone else. I knew everyone's name, and people seemed to like me fine. But I sat at a different lunch table every day, rotating around the room like I was trying to win a musical chairs tournament. After school, I floated in and out of circles of students as they stood on the sidewalk waiting for their rides. I didn't have a place. And therefore I didn't have the status to impress someone like Liza Taylor Smith.

"Here," said Lauren Baker, dropping the note on my desk.

We were getting up to leave Spanish class at the end of the period. I raised my eyebrows, confused. She nodded her head at the note as if to say, *I am leaving this with you, but you deserve no further explanation from me concerning its contents. Read it for yourself.*

I looked down at what was lying on my desk. Based on its dimensions—slightly larger than a credit card, about a centimeter tall—I guessed it was a standard-sized sheet of notebook paper that had been folded once, twice, and then thrice. On the faceup side was written a single word in light blue glitter-gel ink: *Josh.*

I swiped the note off my desk and stuffed it in the front pocket of my capri-length shorts.

As I walked to my locker between Spanish and Honors Biology, I wondered what could be written in this note. I had never been given a note at school before, let alone a note from a girl like Lauren Baker, who was both hot and popular. What could it possibly say? What would she have to tell me that was so important it had to be passed, quietly, almost secretly, in a folded sheet of notebook paper with my name written on it?

Chapter 7

–– – – – – – – ––

I waited to read the note until after I got home from school. I didn't want to read it in public in case its contents turned out to be, you know, emotionally disturbing or something. I went into my bedroom and shut the door, then sat down at my desk, unfolding the piece of paper one crease at a time, my hands shaking almost as much as they had when Mr. Glick popped that quiz. Sparkly blue handwriting took up the entire page. I scanned to the end, expecting to see a signature that said *Lauren*. After all, Lauren Baker was the one who had handed me the note. She must have written it, too, right?

But no. It said no such thing. In fact, there was not one but *two* names written at the end of the letter: *Liza Taylor*.

Liza Taylor? Had written me a letter? Me? Josh Sundquist? There was no way this was real. It was too good to be true. I looked up from my desk and out the window, and then at the door, as if I expected someone to jump out and say that I had been pranked.

But the door remained closed and my room remained quiet. I took a deep breath and dove into the note, savoring each word, each sparkly handwritten letter.

Dear Josh, it began. As I read, my mind kept interrupting me with screams of *Is this really happening?*

The letter went on to explain that she knew we had not met yet.

(Um, seriously? *She knows who I am?*)

But that she was really looking forward to meeting me because, see, her Bible study leader from Young Life had told her all about me, about how I had been diagnosed with cancer as a child, how I had lost my leg.

(Wait, *what*? She already *knows my secret*? All hope is lost!)

Her Bible study leader also told her how my faith in God had gotten me through such a difficult time, and how that faith continued to sustain me today.

Liza Taylor concluded by saying she was inspired and impressed by my faith, and it just really encouraged her to know that, like, another one of her classmates had such a great relationship with God. She hoped we would be able to meet soon.

It was signed simply *Liza Taylor*.

I read the entire note again and again, soaking up every word. It was like taking a shower under drops of bliss. All the happiness washed over me, soaking through to the bone. Liza Taylor had written me! She wanted to meet me! She was impressed with my faith!

Not only that, but she already knew that I had one leg—which I was a little weirded out to discover, since most people at school didn't know yet—and even with this knowledge, *she still wanted to meet me.* My disability did not reduce her opinion of me; in fact, based on the note, it seemed like it actually made her think more highly of me.

That Liza Taylor was in a Bible study was itself a shocking development. Liza Taylor Smith was a Christian! Just like me! Which meant...I could date her! She could be my first real girlfriend!

No sooner had the thought entered my mind, however, than the Rule returned to smack me in the face: No dating until you are sixteen years old.

Mom and Dad had made an exception and allowed me to date Sarah Stevens because she was a family friend. They knew her. She and I had grown up together. But they didn't know Liza Taylor Smith. That she was in a Bible study would not be enough to convince them. To Mom and Dad, she was just some random girl from public school, meaning she was most likely a corrupting seductress or closet Wiccan, Bible study member or not.

I sighed and stared out the window. I was so close! So close to not only meeting Liza Taylor Smith, but dating her! I mean, it said it right there in the letter. *She wanted to meet me.*

That's when I got an idea. I might not be allowed to go on dates, plural, but maybe I could persuade Mom and Dad to let me go on just one. Specifically, to the homecoming dance. It was coming up in a couple of weeks. And since homecoming was a special occasion, closely supervised by chaperones, maybe they'd make an exception to the no-dating rule and let me attend.

I suggested as much at dinner, and they agreed to pray about it. That was a start, at least.

The next evening I brought it up again.

"So, what about homecoming?"

"We can discuss it after dinner," said Dad.

I was eager to hear their answer. "Why not now?"

Mom and Dad glanced at each other.

"Not in front of your younger brothers," said Dad, nodding at Matthew and Luke.

It wasn't until dinner had been finished, the dishes cleared, and my brothers ushered safely out of earshot into the family room with the door closed that I got my answer.

Dad began, "I'm sorry, Joshua, but we have decided not to make an exception"—my shoulders slumped and I let out an exasperated sigh—"to our rule. You're not allowed to date until you're sixteen. And that includes school dances."

"But why does it matter? It's just a dance. I can ask some girl..." Obviously, I would not be asking *some girl*—no, I wanted to ask a very specific girl with three words in her name, but no use telling Mom and Dad that. "...as a friend."

"We just don't think it's safe," Mom said.

"Safe? Like I'm gonna pull a muscle while dancing?"

"No." She looked uncomfortable.

"What then?"

Dad jumped in. "We've heard that a lot of girls get... um..."

I raised my eyebrows.

"Well..." Dad was struggling.

"Yes?" I demanded.

"Pregnant. At the homecoming dance, that is."

Mom's eyelids widened slightly at the mere mention of the p-word, the ultimate embarrassment for any Christian parent, a sin that brought irreversible shame upon any good churchgoing family.

"Oh, come on!" I said. "Pregnant? You think I'm going to have *sex* at the dance?"

"Keep your voice down, please," said Mom, nodding her head at the door to the family room.

"No," said Dad. "We do not think you will. But we don't want to put you in a place of temptation, either."

"A place of temptation? Dad, there are going to be, like, hundreds of kids there. How could I possibly get someone pregnant?"

"Maybe before or after—"

"I can't drive!" I interrupted. "You are going to have to drive me to pick her up and drop her off anyway. In between that we'll be at a dance chaperoned by, like, an army of teachers and parents!"

"True," Dad conceded. "I guess you will be supervised...."

Mom gave him a look.

"But that doesn't change the fact that you aren't allowed to go," added Dad, returning his tone from thoughtful back to this-is-our-final-decision.

"Dad, this is completely absurd." I directed my arguments at Dad, because he was the less strict one. If someone budged, it would be him, not Mom. "You were the one who explained to me where babies come from, remember? I don't recall learning anything about babies coming from people dancing. It's not going to just accidentally happen at the dance."

"Joshua, you are too young to understand, but hormones can be very powerful."

"Explain it. Explain to me how my date could get pregnant."

"Teenagers with hormones can be very creative," he said. "I don't know, exactly. Maybe in a classroom or something. You sneak off with your date—"

"Are you being serious right now? This isn't a joke?"

Dad put his hand up in a stop sign. "That's enough. Our decision is final."

"Ugghhh! You guys are ridiculous!" I pulled my chair from the table as violently as I could and hopped over to my crutches, which were leaning against the wall. I stormed out of the room and went to my bedroom and slammed the door. Sliding open my nightstand drawer, I lifted out the note from Liza Taylor. Then I crumpled it up and threw it on the floor.

Chapter 8

— — — — — — — — — —

A few days after I had to miss homecoming, I was standing outside at the end of the school day, waiting for Mom to pick me up, when I was approached by a college-aged guy wearing a trucker hat and cowboy shirt.

"What's up, bro?" he said, offering a fist bump. "What's your name?"

"I'm Josh."

"Word. They call me Miller."

"Nice to meet you."

"So listen, you should come out to club tonight." He handed me a photocopied flier. "It's gonna be mad fun."

"Cool, thanks."

He walked away to find his next target. I examined the flier. It was a hand-drawn map to someone's house that read YOUNG LIFE CLUB, 7 PM.

My mind pinged, alerting me to a connection between this flier and Liza Taylor Smith. What was the connection?

I thought for a second. Oh yeah, her note! She had said she heard about me from her Young Life leader. Bingo. My chance to finally meet Liza Taylor had literally just been handed to me.

I'd never been to Young Life, but I'd heard of it. It was a Christian organization, sort of a youth group for public schools, led by local college students and other volunteers. The religious affiliation made it an easy sell to Mom and Dad.

That night, Dad dropped me off at the address on Miller's map. I got out of the van and spotted Liza Taylor almost instantly. As promised, she was holding court with a circle of guys, all upperclassmen, all football players.

I didn't want to interrupt, so instead of butting into the

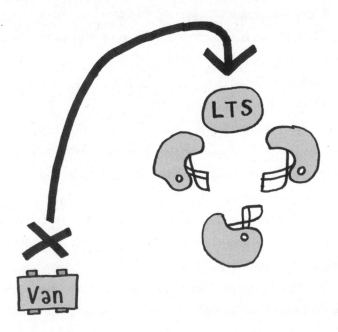

circle, I perched politely just behind Liza Taylor and waited to see if she would notice me.

I guess she eventually felt my breath on her neck or something, and she turned around to face me. I didn't say anything, just waited for her to place me.

"You're Josh Sundquist!"

"Yup!"

"I'm Liza Taylor!"

"I know," I said.

"This is so cool! I didn't know you came to Young Life!"

"It's my first time."

"Well, I'm so glad you're here!"

Then, silence.

We were nearing the point at which a conversational pause turns into awkwardness when the door to the basement burst open and Miller stepped out.

"Everyone inside!" he bellowed.

"Okay, maybe I'll talk to you after club?" Liza Taylor offered.

"Yeah, okay, cool," I concurred.

Everyone funneled through the door into the basement. The furniture had been cleared out to provide ample floor seating. Everyone was gathering on the carpet with their groups of friends. Not having a crew of my own, I sat alone behind the farthest row in the back of the room. There's a big difference between knowing everyone's name and having a group of friends that counts you as one of its members.

Sitting on the floor with a prosthesis like mine is a little awkward. The hip joint doesn't rotate in, so you can't sit cross-legged as most people would in a crowded situation like this. You have to sort of recline, legs out in front of you, palms planted behind you. So you take up a conspicuous amount of floor space, which is especially annoying when you want to be invisible so no one notices that you are sitting by yourself.

Miller jumped up in front of the room.

"*What's up, club?*" he screamed, drawing wild applause. He high-fived a few people in the front row.

"I thought we'd start off tonight with a little... *competition!*"

The promise of competition elicited another round of cheering.

"In honor of the fall holiday known as Thanksgiving, a.k.a. Turkey Day, we are going to have a pumpkin race!"

Although I wasn't sure what a pumpkin race was, just the word "race" gave me an instant flashback to my childhood. When I was seven, I won a blue ribbon in the homeschool science fair for an experiment in which I proved that sprinting at my top speed (which the judges agreed, based on the data I had recorded, was indeed very fast) increased my heart rate compared to when I was walking. I loved to run races back when I had two legs.

"Here's how it works. In a minute we're gonna go back outside, and three competitors will line up at the starting line. They will run out and around the big tree in the front yard. First one across the finish line wins. Oh yeah—and they will be wearing one of these on each foot!"

He produced a pumpkin from the floor in front of him and held it aloft with one hand. The crowd went crazy. Holding the stem of the pumpkin with his other hand, he lifted off a circular top section that had been precut from the pumpkin and showed us the orangey innards through the hole.

"You just take your shoe and sock off and then"—he dropped the pumpkin stem and plunged that hand into the pumpkin—"put your foot right up in there!" He removed his hand to show that it was covered up to his forearm with pumpkin seeds and bright orange strings of pumpkin guts. An *eww*-that's-so-gross laugh erupted in the basement. He set the pumpkin down.

"Now, tonight before club started, three people came up to me and they were like, 'Miller, can I *please* be in tonight's competition!'" This drew a knowing laugh. He pulled a slip of paper out of his pocket. As he read each name, there was a smattering of applause.

"...and Josh Sundquist!"

Liza Taylor, who was sitting in the front, was one of the first to turn around and look at me. She smiled. I felt heat rising to my face.

I wondered how Miller knew my last name. Maybe he had gotten it from Liza Taylor. Or maybe from Liza Taylor's Bible study leader.

But it didn't really matter how he had found out,

because he had—that was over and done with—and now I had to deal with this impossibly uncomfortable situation. Other than Liza Taylor, none of my classmates knew I was missing a leg. If they had known, they would not be clapping; they would be wondering, as I was now, whether it was possible to do this competition with a prosthesis on.

I considered it: I could take the shoe off my artificial leg, though doing so was quite difficult and usually required two hands or the use of a shoehorn. But even if I did get my shoe off, my ankle did not have enough forward flexion to fit through that hole in the top of the pumpkin. In the end, though, none of that mattered, because I simply couldn't run with my prosthesis, pumpkin shoe or not, because the artificial leg didn't swing through fast enough.

I sat still by myself on the floor while everyone made their way outside for the race. I was about to break both my rules: I was going to be a burden on Miller by telling him I couldn't compete, and I was going to identify myself as different when everyone started to wonder why I had dropped out.

Outside, the other two competitors were already clad in their pumpkin footwear. I shuffled over to Miller.

"You ready to gourd up, bro?" he asked.

"Yeah, that's what I need to talk to you about," I said. I leaned my head toward the street, indicating we should turn to face away from the group. "I can't do it. I, um...I have...I have an artificial leg." I glanced down at my leg, which was covered with a pair of pants.

"Oh, bro, I'm so sorry," said Miller. He did indeed

look really sorry, though not so much sympathetic sorry as what-have-I-done horrified sorry. .

"It's all right. I lost it a long time ago."

"No, I'm sorry about calling you up for this race. I had no idea."

"It's cool. Sorry I can't, you know, compete."

"If you want, you can be in another one of tonight's skits. Next we're doing a competition where you put panty hose over your head and have to eat a can of pumpkin pie filling through it—can you do that?"

Can I eat pumpkin pie? This was why I didn't like for people to know I had a fake leg. Once they did, they assumed I wasn't able to do much of anything.

"Sure."

I looked back at the other students, all of whom were monitoring my conversation with Miller. Had they figured out my secret? I searched for Liza Taylor Smith's face in the crowd, but I couldn't find it.

After that night, I saw her on occasion at school. But everything had changed; it had become impossible to believe she could be interested in me, even in my most optimistic of daydreams. During our brief conversations in the hall at school, as I tried to maintain eye contact, fighting the visual gravity of her perfect body, I was distracted by my assumption that *she* was distracted. I was sure she must be replaying her memory of the Young Life meeting, thinking about how I couldn't participate in the pumpkin relay because my own body was irrevocably broken.

HYPOTHESIS

Subject may have held romantic attraction for me, as evidenced by handwritten correspondence written with sparkly pen.

Further investigation is required to determine for certain.

INVESTIGATION

Chapter 9

— — — — — — — — —

Let's be honest here: I'd always been intimidated by Liza Taylor. I mean, even after I was finally allowed to date girls when I was sixteen, I never asked her out. Why? She seemed out of my league. Sure, I still saw her around at school from time to time, but after I had gotten into the swing of things at public school, after I understood the social hierarchy and where I fit in it, I never considered dating her.

So how could I ask her to have coffee with me ten years later, even if the reasons were entirely scientific? Even if I merely wanted to determine whether she had had any interest in me back in freshman year? Even if I just wanted to clear things up for myself, to get the story of my life all straightened out?

But fate intervened. I went to the mall to do some last-minute Christmas shopping, and I happened to run into her in front of Bath & Body Works. Even as we hugged hello, the artificial chemical-based reproductions of mountain breezes and ocean mists wafting in through my nostrils, I felt my blood filling up with adrenaline. To compensate for my nervousness, which can often lead to side effects like stuttering and/or looking down at the ground, I overcorrected with way too much enthusiasm.

"Man, I can't believe we just ran into each other like this!" I exclaimed.

"Yeah, crazy."

"I haven't seen you since high school graduation!"

Each of my sentences ended in an exclamation mark.

"Yeah, I guess you're right."

She had the same droopy eyelids, the same inviting smile. My mind was going a million miles a minute, racing through the questions I had for her, the things I've always wanted to know: Why did she write me that note? Did she have a crush on me? Was she disappointed I never asked her out?

I made an attempt to turn the conversation in the direction of my investigation.

"I always look back on high school and wish I'd spent more time hanging out with you," I said. "You were one of the coolest people in our grade."

"Oh, thanks," she said, in a tone like she was embarrassed. But she wasn't blushing. It was only an act, a well-trained response to compliments by a girl who got them all the time. Either that, or I was just making her uncomfortable.

Whatever, I had to take the risk. I had to find out if she had liked me. So I pushed the conversation to the breaking point.

"Certainly," I added, with all the sincerity I could muster to compensate for the cheesiness of what I was about to say, "you were one of the most beautiful girls in our grade."

"Well...thanks..." she said, actually blushing this time. I clenched up, hoping against all odds that she would respond with something about how I was supercute, too, and remember that note she wrote me? She totally had a crush on me back in high school, and what was I doing tonight for dinner?

"You were...*certainly*..." She struggled for words. "One of the most *interesting* guys in our grade."

The word "interesting" came out of her mouth so slowly and carefully it sounded like the screech of nails on a chalkboard. It was shudder-inducing: The best word in her vocabulary to describe me was..."interesting." "Interesting" is the word you use to describe the color of month-old Chinese takeout noodles in your refrigerator. It's the word you use to describe your superweird aunt and uncle who live in a bombproof nuclear-fallout shelter with a stash of automatic weapons and a twenty-year supply of canned goods.

I briefly considered asking her about the note, asking her why she had written it if I had been merely "interesting."

But I realized that if this was how she felt about me, she wouldn't even remember the note. I mean, let's be honest: A girl writes hundreds of notes during her high school career. She only remembers a few of them once she's an adult. And the ones she remembers are certainly not those written to boys she found "interesting."

There was nothing else to discover here. That one word answered all my questions.

"Okay, cool, well, nice to see you," I said, faking a smile.

"You, too."

And we walked our separate ways, annoying ding-a-ling holiday music echoing all around us.

FRANCESCA
MARCELO

BACKGROUND

Chapter 10

— — — — — — — —

Geometry class, first day of spring semester in eleventh grade. The room was filling up and there was one desk left open. The one right in front of me. The seconds were ticking down before the bell would ring. Somebody was going to walk in and take this seat, and I would spend the rest of the semester staring at the back of the head belonging to this particular somebody.

Please, God, let it be a hot girl.

The reason I cared so much about who sat in this seat was that I had just recently turned sixteen. Sixteen, meaning I was finally allowed to date. I had a pretty sweet ride (a Toyota Camry, one year older than I was) and a girlfriend-shaped hole in my heart. That's why, sitting there at my desk, I was praying that whoever would fill that seat might also happen to be, you know, girlfriend-shaped.

Then, in walked Francesca Marcelo. Let me say that again in case you missed it:

Francesca. Marcelo. Walked. Into. The. Room.

Yes, people, there is a God.

Francesca was hot. Really hot. But she wasn't queen-bee, alpha-female-cheerleader hot; she was art-class, vegetarian, hemp-jewelry hot. Unlike most girls her age, she had this aura that suggested she'd already found herself and was content with what she'd found. She was cool enough to hang out with the popular kids but chose to merely float in and out of their circles, sometimes gracing their lunch table or weekend parties with her presence, sometimes not. As far as I knew, she'd never had a boyfriend. She just made guys nervous—even the popular guys, the ones with cool cars manufactured in the current decade.

As I said, Francesca was hot. But I was attracted to her because she was more than that. She was a mystery, an enigma, a challenge. I might not have understood pretty girls, but I did understand challenges.

But I couldn't carry on a conversation longer than *Hey, did you do that fun homework assignment yet?* To which she'd just say, *Ummm, fun?*

Winter turned into late spring. Then it was almost summer. I knew I had to make a move. But if it was so difficult to talk to her about normal things that I knew a lot about (read: math homework), how could I ever will myself to articulate a series of words that would ask her out and therefore risk rejection?

The same people who tell you *The worst thing she can do is say no* will also tell you *Even if she does say no, she is rejecting you only based on surface reasons. She doesn't know the real you.* Surface reasons like what, exactly? My personality? That I'm not funny enough, or confident enough, or interesting enough, or intelligent enough? Or do these surface reasons concern the way I look? That I am not handsome enough, or thin enough, or muscular enough, or that I have an abnormally shaped body, or that my haircut isn't expensive enough or my clothes stylish enough?

Are these the "surface reasons" we are talking about here? Surface or not, take away my personality and appearance and I'm not sure what is left. I'm not sure what the "real me" would be apart from them. But I know one thing: There aren't a lot of girls who would date a guy with no personality. Or body. Surface or not, I'm of the opinion that these things do matter, at least to some degree, and therefore a rejection of them can't be trivialized.

So I reject your attempts to downplay the pain of rejection, well-meaning advice givers. You can't rationalize this one away. I mean, you can try. You can try to say that it's a numbers game, that you need to get X number of rejections before you finally get a yes. Or that every person has a preset chemical affinity for people with other predetermined chemical characteristics, an explanation that would in theory at least suggest you can make a formula for it, that fate has already been determined by the inevitability of the numbers. You can try to approach it this way. I know because believe me, I have.

But this is where you run smack into the outer limits of numbers and theory and enter the domain of emotions, an irrational wasteland of dangerously unpredictable weather patterns. You can throw all the numbers at it that you want, you can shout theories all day long, you can draw graphs and make flowcharts until you run out of paper, but in the end, rejection is just pure pain, and fighting emotion with logic is like bringing a calculator to a knife fight. You're going to get stabbed in the heart, and there's nothing your precious numbers can do to protect you.

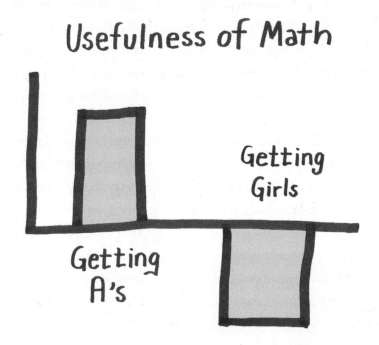

Chapter 11

— — — — — — — — —

Like cancer, war, and acne, the best way to avoid the pain of rejection is to take steps to stop it before it starts. That's what I was thinking about on the last day of my junior year of high school. Francesca and I had lockers on opposite ends of the same first-floor hallway. After the last exam period was finished, I could see that she was cleaning out her locker, getting ready to go home for the summer—taking down photos and Post-it notes from her BFFs, all that. This was it. My last chance.

"Hey," I said.

"Hi," she said.

"Good times in geometry, huh?"

"Yeah."

"No more geometry now, though."

"No, I guess not."

I took a deep breath and then unleashed the line that I had been rehearsing all morning.

"So...we should hang out sometime."

Boom. I want to pause here and acknowledge how that line may have blown your mind with its sheer awesomeness. If you need to take a break before you keep reading, I'll understand.

Okay. Hopefully that was a long enough break.

We should hang out sometime is so perfect because it's nearly impossible to say no to. That's how I first thought of it: I was looking for a way to ask out Francesca without any possibility of rejection.

Let me explain why it's rejection-proof. First of all, it's a statement, not a question. If you ask a girl a yes-or-no question like *Do you want to hang out sometime?*, you are opening the door to rejection. But by making a statement instead of posing a question, you are just sharing an opinion. And any well-mannered person knows it's rude to disagree with someone else's opinion to his or her face. For example, let's say you walk up to a girl and say, *I really like Tuesdays.* What's she going to say? *No, I don't think so?* Of course not. She has to acknowledge that you've shared an opinion. *Oh . . . yeah.*

The second reason this line is so chock-full of win is that it's general rather than specific. If you say, *We should hang out next Thursday at seven o'clock*, all she has to do is say, *Oh, sorry, that's when my favorite Bravo reality show,* Next Top Singing Chef Model, *comes on.* But by using the word "sometime," you are setting such a vague and general parameter that her only way out of it is to claim she's already booked for every hour of the rest of her life, which would obviously be a lie. And if she's a liar, she's not good enough for you anyway, is she?

Finally, the line sounds casual, maybe even platonic. You're not asking her to dinner and a movie or a walk on

Statements That Can't Be Rejected

Today is Tuesday.

Blue is my favorite color.

I am hungry.

We Should Hang Out Some-time

Pickup Lines

I lost my number. Can I have yours?

Can I be your derivative so I can lie tangent to your curves?

Want to rearrange the alphabet and put "U" and "I" together?

the beach at sunset or some other activity with a blinking neon DATE! sign on it. You just want to hang out, like, you know, friends. And if you're just trying to be friends, it would be impolite to say no.

So I threw down the line *We should hang out sometime.* And Francesca was like, "Yeah, totally."

"Okay, cool," I said. "I'll give you a call."

So that's what I did, just called her out of nowhere a week later. How'd I get her number? I looked up her parents in the phone book. Totally not weird.

"Hey, it's Josh Sundquist. Remember me?" In high school, I always opened my calls to girls this way. Just to make sure.

"Um, yeah, of course."

"So when are we going to hang out?"

"Well...whenever," she said in a surprisingly agreeable tone.

"How about tomorrow?"

"All right."

"You ever played golf at the par-three course in Bridgewater?"

"No."

"You know about it?"

"Yeah, I think so."

"Well, it's awesome."

"Okay."

"So you want to go there?"

"Sure."

I added, to clarify, "With me?"

"Sure."

The next day, I washed the outside and vacuumed the inside of my seventeen-year-old Camry. I got one of those cardboard Christmas tree things to hang from my rearview mirror, too. New-car scent. Which, as it turned out, smelled disgusting.

I will never, ever forget how Francesca looked when she was walking down the stairs at her house. I had just rung the bell, and I could see through the window in the front door as she appeared at the top of the staircase. She was wearing sky-blue nylon surfer-girl shorts with a white spaghetti-strap top. The straps on the shirt crossed diagonally in the front, forming an X beneath her neck. Her

LysoL

Public restroom

"New- Car Scent="

short brown hair bounced with each step as she descended. She took my breath away. Literally. And in the instinctive human response to not being able to breathe, I started panicking. Our date was going to be a disaster of awkward silences and nervous stuttering. There was just no way I could talk to her. Not without hyperventilating, at least.

Just as she opened the door and stepped onto the porch, I thought of a lifesaving idea.

"Hi," she said, smiling.

"Hey," I said. "So I was...uh...wondering."

She raised her eyebrows while I composed my words.

"Do you have any, you know, like, awesome music we could listen to in the car?"

Boo-ya! Such a good idea, right? If there were any

awkward pauses on the car ride, I could just drum my fingers on the steering wheel and it would seem like I was entranced by her music instead of running low on preprepared conversation topics.

See, when it comes to girls, I've always believed in being prepared. You can't leave something as important as conversation up to chance. Fact: The first time I ever called a girl, at age thirteen, I wrote a page-long list of possible conversational questions before dialing her number from the phone book. I took notes on her answers. I intended to refer back to them when we started dating once I was sixteen. As it turned out, by that time she had a boyfriend. But I still had the notes.

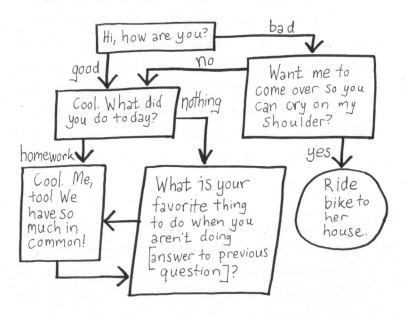

So anyway, I asked Francesca for a CD. She was like, "Sure, hold on." She returned with an Ani DiFranco CD.

"She's my favorite."

That was Francesca speaking, not me. Because I had never heard of Ani DiFranco. Ani DiFranco's songs, as it turns out, are best described as guitar picking played as background music while Ani, an angry, dreadlocked feminist lesbian, spouts diatribes against men. The music created that perfect mood of politically charged man-hating that I always go for on a first date. Ladies, if you're looking to start a date off right, you can't go wrong with Ani.

"What do you think?" asked Francesca of the music.

"Oh yeah," I said neutrally. "Really...interesting."

Par-three golf on a municipal golf course is an ideal first date. First of all, it's free. That's key when you're sixteen years old and your primary source of income is your allowance, which has never been adjusted for inflation.

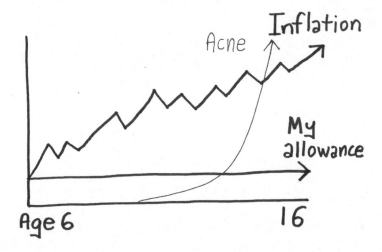

Things were going well for Francesca and me—I made some jokes, she laughed at at least one of them, and most importantly, there were zero awkward pauses—until the sixth hole.

That's when disaster struck.

Chapter 12

— — — — — — — — —

To understand exactly how this date fell apart, you need to know two things. Number one—as mentioned, this was a par-three golf course. In case you've never heard of par three, let me inform you: It's basically extended Putt-Putt. You could take your local mini-golf course, get rid of the ten-foot-tall windmill, add in a few sand traps, move the holes back a foot or two, and you're done. You've got par-three golf. Number two—I was wearing my artificial leg, and prosthetic limbs come preprogrammed out of the box to malfunction at the worst possible moments in your entire life.

So I took this shot off the sixth tee, and it was perfect. It arced up into the air, pausing for a moment, suspended at its vertex, and then dropped down onto the green. It was a beautiful parabola, a perfect $y = -x^2$ arc. Stopped maybe twenty-four inches from the hole. I got all excited and started jumping around, because I figured that a display of athletic prowess of this magnitude would totally make Francesca fall desperately in love with me.

Anyway, one second I was pumping my fist in celebration and the next I was falling backward in slow motion, arms flailing behind my head. I landed on my back and glanced up to see Francesca staring at me, all deer-in-the-headlights. I've seen the look a million times. All right, maybe not a million, but a few. Because let's face it, I've fallen down before. Fake legs aren't the easiest things to walk with. And people never know what you're supposed to do when the one-legged guy falls down. Are you allowed to laugh at him? Should you help him up? Maybe take him to therapy? Francesca did one of those half-laugh, half-sympathy things you do when you see a cute little baby trip and land on his diaper while he's learning to walk.

"Are you all—ha—I mean are you—hee—all right?"

"Yeah, I think so."

But I wasn't all right. I was watching my dreams of an impending make-out session vanish into thin air. And not only were my dreams vanishing, my nightmares were coming true: My disability was going to ruin my chances with Francesca.

I stood up and brushed off the grass clippings, telling myself things couldn't possibly get worse.

And that's when things got worse.

I looked down and discovered that the foot on my artificial leg was turned backward. Like, it was literally facing

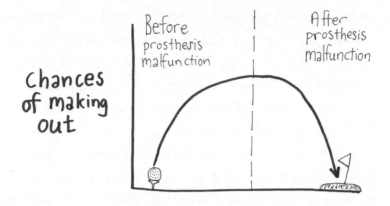

Chances of making out

Before prosthesis malfunction

After prosthesis malfunction

the opposite direction of my real foot. I glanced at Francesca. She wasn't laughing anymore. The awkwardness level was off the charts, well beyond the scale of any normal measurement of social discomfort. But at least Francesca knew I had a prosthesis. You can't imagine the horror on the faces of the other golfers as they stared at a leg apparently so severely fractured that the foot was now capable of rotating 180 degrees. The other golfers were undoubtedly whipping out their cell phones to call 911.

Hi, nine-one-one? I have a serious golfing injury to report.... A young man fell down and when he stood up his foot was turned backward.... I don't know how it's possible, either, but I'm telling you that's how it looks from my angle.... Yes, a female companion... No, based on her body language right now, I'd assume they'll never be more than just friends....

It's strange to walk in the direction opposite of where one of your feet is pointing. And I imagine it looks even stranger. Still, I managed to hobble over to a tree by the side of the fairway. I started kicking the tree with my artificial leg, trying to pop the foot back into place. When I was too out of breath to continue kicking, I paused to examine my progress. None. Zero. The foot was still facing backward. I needed more leverage. I began kicking again, spinning with full roundhouse kicks so my artificial foot struck the tree at eye level. At this point, I was sure the other golfers were looking at each other and saying, *This guy has some* serious *anger management problems.*

I looked down and saw that my foot was finally pointing in the same direction as the rest of my body. That was the good news. The bad news was that I had chopped down the tree. Not literally chopped it down the way loggers do with chain saws, like, *Timberrrrrr!* It was more like the way smaller trees look after a hurricane has come through and they're bent parallel to the ground. So, yeah. Definitely left a big carbon footprint that day.

Francesca—who was, in retrospect, probably something of a conservationist—and a small group of similarly minded onlookers all just stood there, jaws hanging open in silence, as I walked over to my ball with both feet facing proudly forward and putted it in for a birdie. I pumped my fist and smiled like things were going great. Trying to keep up appearances. Keep the date alive. Even with this hole-in-two, though, I knew my chances with Francesca were ruined. The contortions on her face while I was destroying that young sapling had said it all: *This is awkward.*

On the way home, we listened to Ani again. This time I connected. With her anger. She is so deep, this Ani DiFranco, I thought. She sees the world for what it truly is. A cruel, dark place that chews up those who are different and spits them out again.

I pulled into Francesca's driveway and parked my car in front of the garage. I didn't bother to turn off the idling engine. This good-bye, I expected, would not last long.

"Thanks for coming," I said, breaking the silence.

"I had fun," she said. "We should hang out more this summer."

I opened my mouth to say "see you later" or whatever I had planned to say before she spoke, but my voice caught when I recognized the tonality of her words. She actually sounded like she wanted to see me again.

"Okay, well, yeah, I'll see you soon then."

Chapter 13

———————

It was a month into the summer, and I had been coming over to Francesca's house once or twice a week to play pool in her basement. After I beat her,[4] we'd sit on the porch swing in the backyard and talk. Or I'd take her to Jess's Quick Lunch downtown. All of which is to say, by the time we went hiking we were pretty skilled at talking to each other, which was good since the drive to the trailhead was longer than I remembered—about two hours, or two and a half Ani DiFranco CDs.

Hiking down to the base of the falls is pretty easy because you're doing just that. Hiking down. You park on Skyline Drive in Shenandoah National Park and then you descend for four miles of switchbacks, worrying the whole time about the moment when you will be sitting on that rock overlooking the waterfall and you will turn your head

---

[4] It's never been clear to me whether you're supposed to let a girl win or not. I went with not.

sideways and purse your lips and close your eyes and move in for the kill. But if you close your eyes first, how will you know where, exactly, to move? Maybe you move in first and then close your eyes? And when do you insert your tongue into her mouth?

The base of the falls was just how I remembered it from when I went there with my youth group in eighth grade, when I climbed on top of that rock and that guy told me to bring a girl back here someday: heavily wooded with trees and shrubbery and shadowed by a towering rock face, with a backyard-pool-sized swimming hole underneath. There was no one else there. It was like our own perfect, private oasis in the forest.

I had been hoping that Francesca would wear a bikini that day, but she was sporting a modest green-and-black one-piece.

Much more disappointing was that she wouldn't swim in the pool underneath the falls.

"It's too cold," she said.

She just stood up to her ankles and watched while I jumped off a low ledge into the water, trying to splash her with irresistible fun vibes. But she didn't budge. She just smiled and said something about how this all looked like a movie, which made me realize that if this were really a movie, my character would be expected to grab her around the waist and pull her into the water. She would shriek and scream in protest, but deep down she would love it. Then we'd splash each other and giggle like schoolchildren, and she'd start trying to dunk me, and then I would fake like I had drowned by breathing through a straw made out of bamboo, and she'd freak out and start crying and her wrists would hang limp while she flapped her hands, and then I'd pop out of the water and surprise her and she'd laugh and then we'd kiss. And maybe that's what she was hoping would happen. After all, why else would she strip down to her swimsuit and stand at the edge of the water like that? I started to swim toward her so I could pull her in, but while I did so I made the mistake of thinking. Then I stopped and treaded water. I couldn't do it. There was simply too much risk. Risk that she'd be annoyed by the cold water. Risk that she would find me grabbing her around the waist inappropriate. Risk that my balance, standing with one leg on the slick rocks, wouldn't be stable enough to topple her. Risk that it would be awkward. Risk that she didn't like me. I shook my head, wishing I were in a movie instead of in my brain.

"What?" she asked.

"Nothing."

I climbed out of the water and picked up my crutches. I thought about putting my shirt back on but decided to keep it off in the hope she would be impressed by what I imagined were the chiseled muscles of my sixteen-year-old chest. This, I would soon discover, was a massive tactical error. But not for the reasons you probably think.

"Come on, I want to show you something."

We walked in our swimsuits and bare feet up the steep, rooted path. At the top, we came to the rock, and again I hesitated—not about kissing her, but about simply sitting down. What if I sat down and she didn't sit beside me? I looked at her. I looked at the rock. No, couldn't do it. Too big a risk. So I just stood there surveying the stupid trees below and thinking how stupid it was that I couldn't even bring myself to take the risk of sitting on a stupid rock and what was wrong with my stupid brain, until suddenly she sat down on the rock and looked up at me like I was supposed to join her. I smiled and bit my lower lip.

"What?" she asked.

"Nothing."

I set my crutches down and then sat beside her, beads of water rolling down my back. Phase one was complete.

But I wasn't sure how to initiate phase two, the kiss. Maybe I could do so by telling the story of how I first came here three years ago, how ever since then I had thought this would be a perfect place for, you know, a first kiss?

"I came to this rock a few years ago. I've always wanted to come back." Upon its telling, I realized the story was both shorter and less effective than I had hoped.

"It's a beautiful view," she offered.

"Yeah."

We were silent for a while, listening to the roar of the waterfall. It was the good kind of silent, though. She breathed in slowly through her nose, taking in the scene. And then she said, thoughtfully, "It smells like pot up here."

I had absolutely no clue what pot smelled like.

"Yeah," I said, sniffing. "It totally does."

Then we were quiet again.

I decided to try another tactic for initiating phase two, the Deep Conversation.

"Let me ask you something," I said.

"Okay."

"Why do you think adults give up on their dreams?"

"Um, I don't know."

"But you know what I'm saying, right? It's like everyone our age wants to change the world or be famous or something, right?"

She shrugged. "Yeah, I guess."

"But most adults don't do any of those things. They just live sort of normal lives. But it's like, they're okay with that. It doesn't bother them."

"I never really thought about it that way."

"Why do you think that is?"

She was quiet for a little bit. "I don't know. I guess people just get busy."

"I guess so."

"What do you think?" she asked.

I didn't know. But I wanted to know. I wanted my life to count. I wanted my dreams to come true. "Yeah, you're probably right. People get busy."

She nodded.

I looked out at the treetops and continued speaking with all the heady profundity that comes with knowing so much and understanding so deeply how the world works. "They get busy with being married and having children and house payments. And then they're old and they missed out on their dreams."

"That's probably it."

"Good thing we're still young."

"Yeah."

"And that we figured that out."

"Yeah."

We were both watching the water zip off the edge just below us. You could taste the mist coming off the falls.

"I want to change the world," I blurted out.

"You do?"

"Yeah. And I'm going to do it, too."

"How?"

"I don't know. But I'm going to."

She looked right in my eyes.

"I believe you," she said, seriously.

We held each other's gaze. Neither of us said anything. Neither of us moved. Neither of us even blinked. I moved my head forward exactly one centimeter. She squinted slightly, questioningly.

This is it, I thought. It's going to happen. My first kiss. Right now.

That's when it hit me: I was wearing a swimsuit. No underwear. No shirt. If I got, you know, excited, which seemed all but certain during my first kiss, it would be about as subtle as a circus tent going up on your next-door neighbor's front lawn. And what would she think? Would she be grossed out and go home and call her friends and tell them about it? Would it be a story that followed me through the halls of my high school until graduation?

"Well, it's getting kind of late," I said, glancing up at the dimming afternoon sky.

Her body jumped involuntarily, as if startled.

"Oh. I guess you're . . . right."

As we hiked all the way back up to the car, I told her about my dream to become a Paralympic ski racer someday. I had learned to ski right after I lost my leg as a kid, and while I was still on chemotherapy I met a former coach of the US Paralympic Team, who told me I had "great potential." Ever since then, ever since that day, I had wanted to race in the Paralympics. I asked her what her dreams were, and she said she didn't have any. I told her she should get some.[5]

"I guess you're right," said Francesca.

Hiking against gravity was significantly slower than

---

[5] Side benefit of dating me: free motivational speeches. It's like friends with benefits where the benefits are inspirational.

hiking with it, as it turned out. The sun set and the trail turned dark under the canopy of a dense pine forest. Interesting, I thought, since we hadn't walked through any dense pine forests on the way down.

"I think we lost the trail," I said.

We examined the bed of pine needles under our feet. There was indeed no trail.

"This is like something out of a horror movie," she said.

I recognized this as my cue to demonstrate bravery.

"Yeah, pretty freaky," I agreed, not bravely at all.

Francesca and I wandered around the woods in the dark, trying to navigate by moonlight and the North Star, something I had learned how to do in Boy Scouts. By

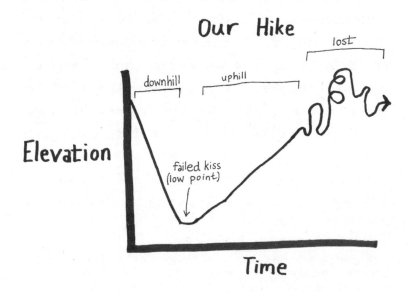

"learned" I don't mean I could actually do it, but that I knew enough big words ("latitude," "equator," "compass," "south by southwest," etc.) to get the orienteering merit badge.[6] So my only real strategy was to keep us walking in the same direction. As long as you go in a straight line, you'll eventually run into the end of the national park, right?

I would later discover that as we wandered, Francesca's dad was calling my house every hour. At one point Francesca's dad said to my dad on the phone, "I just want you to know, even though I'm a little worried right now, there's actually no young man I'd rather have my daughter out with than your son."

Oh, great. Thanks. Just what every teenaged Ani DiFranco fan wants, a guy who has the enthusiastic endorsement of her father.

I'm not sure why parents always liked me when I was growing up. Maybe because I used big words and knew how to do math problems. Maybe they thought cancer made me mature for my age. Maybe because they thought I wouldn't be able to try anything on their daughters since I had a physical disability. Whatever it was, it's safe to say that if girls chose their boyfriends based on who their

---

[6] I'm actually an Eagle Scout. But the only time I ever did orienteering, I got lost and my artificial leg got stuck in some bushes and then it got dark and cold and I had to blow my emergency rescue whistle until the Scout leaders came and found me. Unfortunately, I did not bring such a whistle on my date with Francesca.

parents liked, I could've required resumes and head shots from girls before they would even be eligible for consideration. That's how much the parents liked me. But parental approval doesn't do much for you when you're trying to date high school chicks. In fact, it makes it harder, because deep down every teenaged girl wants to bring home some biker dude with prison tattoos and a tendency to break anything that shatters (beer bottles, windshields, young girls' hearts) just so her dad will flip out.

Eventually, Francesca and I stumbled out of the pine forest onto a road. There were no cars or people in sight.

"This really is just like a horror movie," she said again.

Being that in my family we weren't allowed to watch PG-13-rated movies until we were sixteen, and R-rated movies until we were adults and responsible for our own souls, I had never actually seen a horror movie.

"Yeah," I said. "It totally is."

We followed the pavement in a randomly chosen direction for thirty minutes and eventually found the parking lot, empty except for my car, which was sparkling in the moonlight thanks to a trip to the car wash that morning.

Chapter 14

— - — — — — — — —

About halfway through the summer, I ran into some guys I knew from school. They said they heard Francesca and I had been hanging out. I asked them where they had heard that. They said around. I took this as good news.

One day she called me and we had the following conversation.

"What are you doing this weekend?" she asked.

"Nothing. What are you doing?"

"You ever heard of Pat McGee?"

"I think so. A singer, right?" I said.

"Uh-huh. His band is having a concert up in DC."

"Cool," I said. "You going?"

"I really want to, but my parents said I'm not allowed to drive to DC."

"Bummer."

"I know, huge bummer," she said.

There was a pause. You will be tempted to think I am

making up this next comment to amuse you. Alas, I am not. This is what I actually said.

"Driving in cities is one of the few things my parents let me do," I said. "I've even driven to DC a few times."

There was another pause, as if she was waiting for me to say something else. I filled in the silence with, "So... what are you going to do instead?"

"Nothing, I guess," she said softly.

Sometimes I hear people say that if they could go back in time and relive their lives, they wouldn't change a thing. Obviously, these people have never had a conversation like this one. If only I had a time machine so I could go back to my younger self, slap him in the face, take the phone, and say, *I apologize for this loser's utter stupidity! Hold on a second.*

Then I would put my hand over the mouthpiece, turn to my sixteen-year-old-self, and say, *Dude! She wants you to give her a ride to DC!*

But as of this writing, time machines haven't been invented yet. So this is how the conversation ended, in the timeline of past reality as it currently stands: My former self said he'd call her in the next day or two because "we need to hang out again in the near future," and then he said good-bye and hung up.

Even though I missed the chance to take her to DC for the concert, we did keep hanging out. And over the next few weeks, whenever we were playing pool in her basement, I would think how much I wanted to kiss her. What I needed was the perfect date.

As far as I could tell, the main things girls were looking for in a potential boyfriend were romance and danger. Romance because they grew up wanting to live in a fairy tale, to have a handsome prince rescue them and all that. Danger because...Well, I'm not sure, but it seemed like girls always went for the bad boys, not the nice ones like me. So what I needed was an activity that combined these two pieces. What kind of date would have both romance and danger? One day it just popped into my head: a picnic on top of a skyscraper.

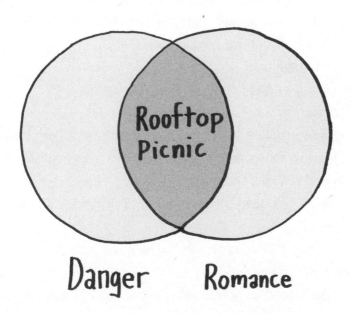

Danger   Romance

No, seriously. That was my plan. Francesca and I would lay down a blanket on the roof and eat up there in the clouds. She'd talk about how scared she was of heights and I'd make fun of her for it. Then we'd kiss, right there on the edge of the skyscraper. Romance. Danger. Together. The two become one.

Unfortunately, we didn't have any skyscrapers in Harrisonburg, but we did have an old office building on Court Square that was probably a good twenty stories tall. That would have to be it. I tracked down the owner, James McHone, at his jewelry store next door. He was skinny and bald, perched on a plush antique chair as if it was a throne.

"A picnic," he said thoughtfully, bringing his knees up to his chest and hugging them. "We might be able to do that. People are always trying to get up there. It's the best view in Harrisonburg, you know!"

"I thought so."

"But it's dangerous," he said cautiously.

"Exactly."

"The problem is that when people go up there on the roof, their shoes get it all dirty." His ring-clad fingers twitched with the thought.

"We don't need to wear shoes," I offered. "We can go in socks."

He nodded. This seemed to be good news to him, so I continued.

"And we'll bring a blanket to sit on. It'll protect your roof."

"Will you be careful?" he asked.

"Yeah, we'll be careful."

He nodded. "Okay, you got it."

"Thanks, James!" I said, slapping him a high five.

"Uncle James," he corrected.

"Right. Thanks, Uncle James!"

"And don't forget that when you're ready to get a ring for this girl—"

"I'm going to come to my uncle James, of course."

I called Francesca that night to tell her about the plan, hoping she'd be as excited about it as I was.

Chapter 15

——————————

"How was your day?" I asked. I was sitting on my parents' bed. We had two phones in our house, one in the kitchen and one in my parents' bedroom. When I wanted privacy, which is to say when I was talking to a girl I liked, I used the one in their bedroom.

"Okay," Francesca said over the phone. "But I had to hang out with Andrew."

"Yikes."

"I just felt bad because I'd told him I was busy like ten times in a row."

Andrew was this other kid from school. He'd been calling Francesca that summer, too. Fortunately for me, Andrew didn't know the "we should hang out sometime" line, which would've stealthily evaded the I'm-too-busy excuses she usually gave him.

"So how was it?" I asked.

"Fine. I guess."

Suddenly I felt a nearly overwhelming urge to ask questions about her date with Andrew. It was like a sneeze welling up inside my nose, desperate to blow its snot load all over the phone. And like a sneeze, I knew that this gossip session would feel oh so good. We would talk about whether Andrew liked her, whether she liked him, whether they'd make a cute couple. *Achoo*. Oh yeah. But I was smart enough by age sixteen to steel myself against this urge with every bit of resistance power I could muster from my puritanical upbringing, because to give in to it would be to commit an unforgivable sin in Francesca's eyes.

Talking about another guy she might be interested in would identify me as friend material. A nice guy. And the only time nice guys finish first is in a race to the Friend Zone.

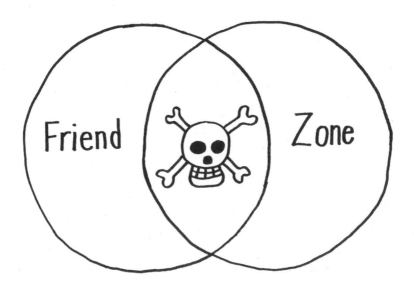

So even though I was supertempted to pursue a line of conversation about Francesca's date with Andrew, I overcame my game-killing instincts and changed the subject.

"Listen, I have something we should do together."

"What?"

"A picnic."

"Sounds fun."

"A picnic...on top of a building."

"What?"

"On a building. Like a picnic on a roof."

"What for?"

Not really the response I was hoping for.

"Because it will be awesome. We'll have a great view, there will be a nice breeze, and it'll be something we can say we did."

She considered it.

"All right, I'm in."

"Yeah?"

"Sure."

I thought I heard her giggle.

"Okay, great. I've got it all set up."

"Sounds fun. I'm excited."

Excited! This date was getting better by the minute.

"Maybe next week?"

Her voice dropped. "Oh," she said.

"What?"

"I'm going on vacation next week."

"How about the week after?"

"It's a two-week vacation. I could the week after that, though."

"No...I'll be on vacation then," I said. "And the next week I'm working at camp."

"And then school starts."

"Bummer."

After we said our good-byes and hung up, I sat silently on my parents' bed for a while. I could already feel it. It was like when you're having a cool dream, like the one where you can fly, and it's everything you ever hoped it would be, but then you realize this is impossible so it must be a dream and you drop out of the sky and wake up. Once school started, I would be reminded of how popular she was, and how, according to the social order of things, I wasn't supposed to be cool enough to go out with her. I would lose my nerve.

Chapter 16

- - - - - - - -

The next time I saw her or even talked to her was indeed a month later, the night before school started. We were at a punk rock show at the local VFW post.

I would roll up to these shows with spiked hair and my totally punk rock necklace, a chain of marble-sized silver balls strung together that I owned solely for these occasions. I was what you'd call a poser. I wasn't even allowed to listen to the music at home. I just liked going to the shows to socialize. And to mosh.

After one particular song, I hopped out of the mosh pit, sweaty and out of breath, and when I picked up my crutches I found Francesca was standing right there in front of me.

"__," she said.

"What?" I said.

"__."

I pointed at my ears and then toward the door that led outside.

We went out to the sidewalk. It was dark and humid, and the music pulsed on the other side of the door. We swapped summaries of our vacations, slipping back into an easy familiarity. I had not expected to see her tonight, but as we talked, the memories of the summer lit up in my mind, and the same rushing swirl of excitement and doubt flooded my awareness. There were some kids making out in the bushes nearby. Should I kiss her? I wanted to. I didn't know if she would kiss back. But if she didn't, at least then I would know. I would know she didn't like me. I jingled my car keys in my hand, trying to fill a conversational void while I worked up the nerve. No. I couldn't do it. School was starting tomorrow. Summer was over. She was popular. I was not. Time to return to reality.

"Well, I'm going home," I said. "Got to get some sleep before first period tomorrow."

"Okay," she said. We hugged. "Good to see you."

When I got home I went to the bathroom to brush my teeth. I looked in the mirror, but I couldn't make eye contact with myself. I had let myself down. Again. It was so stupid! Why couldn't I just step up and, I don't know, be brave or something? I was an embarrassment to myself. And it had to stop. It was time to take a risk. It was time to take action. I looked at myself in the mirror, set my jaw, and nodded.

I got in my car and drove back to the concert. I slammed my car door and marched into the VFW post, waving my already stamped hand at the door guy as I entered. Another band was setting up on the far side of the room. Francesca was sitting against the wall talking to a friend. I was nervous. But I had to do this. Do what? I wasn't sure. But something had to happen, and it had to happen tonight.

"I thought you left," she said when she noticed me standing in front of her. I hoped she had not also noticed that I was shaking from all the adrenaline.

"I did."

Francesca exchanged a look with her friend that I couldn't read. Then she looked back up at me.

"Can I talk to you?" I asked.

"Sure."

"Outside?"

"Okay."

We walked out the door, across the sidewalk, and to the parking lot without saying anything. I sat down on one of those log-shaped cement parking stops. She followed suit, sitting right beside me.

"I just wanted to say..." I began. What, exactly? What was I doing here? Was I trying to kiss her? Tell her something? I squeezed the top of the cement block so she wouldn't be able to see my hand shaking.

"I just wanted to say...that I'm really glad I asked you to play golf at the start of the summer," I said.

Perfect. That was it. All I needed to do was say that,

and now she would look at me and tell me she'd never met a guy like me before and she wanted to be with me forever. And we'd kiss.

"I'm so glad you did," she said.

"And?"

I waited for her to say how much she liked me, how she thought about me every waking moment of every day.

"Yeah, I'm glad you did," she said.

Why wasn't this working? Why wasn't she trying to kiss me or something? Then I realized I myself hadn't really said anything yet. I hadn't made a move.

This was all so much more difficult than I had imagined it would be back when I was brushing my teeth by myself in the safety of my home.

"It's like... you're so cool," I said. "I thought you were this person I could never talk to...."

"People always tell me stuff like that."

"They do?"

"Yeah. I don't understand."

"You're just, I don't know, you're..."

There were so many options, so many ways to say what needed to be said. And they were all there right in front of me, on the tip of my tongue.

But what came out was, "You, and it's like, wow, I can't believe I'm talking to you right now."

I was drowning. Drowning in a raging sea of feelings, coughing and sputtering out desperate, disjointed words while I struggled to keep my head above water. There was a life ring floating right in front of me. All I had to do was reach out and grab it. Tell her how I felt. The problem was, emotional beats rational. Fear trumps logic. Every time.

"Okay, well, I guess I'll see you at school tomorrow," I said.

Not knowing what else to do, in the following weeks I made the very strategic move of never calling her again. We didn't have any classes together fall of senior year, and when I'd pass her in the hallway, each of us exchanging a cheery greeting that ended in an exclamation mark, I'd tell myself that it didn't matter anyway. There was no way a girl like that would ever like a boy like me, right? Right?

Whenever I saw her, I would think back to that night sitting in the parking lot during the concert and wonder: Did I have a chance after all? Was there a possibility that maybe she liked me, just a little bit? When we were sitting there on that rock, was she perhaps feeling a tiny flutter of hope that I would kiss her? If so, was she completely confused—or even hurt—at the end of the summer when I suddenly stopped calling her? Did she think that maybe I was not interested in her in that way, that maybe for some reason I actually wanted to stay in the Friend Zone? Did she wonder if she had done something wrong?

Or maybe she didn't like me after all. Maybe the golf course prosthesis disaster scared her off. Maybe she kept seeing me after that because she was simply too nice to say no.

At any rate, I graduated high school a semester early so I could pursue my dream of being a ski racer. It took a lot of convincing, but eventually my parents gave me permission to move out to Colorado in December and become a full-time athlete, training every day on the mountain at Winter Park and traveling around the western United States and Canada for competitions. During the ski season, I didn't think much about girls. All I thought about, really, was skiing. And by the time I came back to Harrisonburg at the end of the ski season, it was late March. It had been so long since I had talked to Francesca that I knew I'd never get another chance with her.

HYPOTHESIS

Subject behavior suggests Francesca may have had romantic attraction toward me, but due to my awkward behavior and fear-induced reluctance to initiate mouth-to-mouth contact, she lost interest over time.

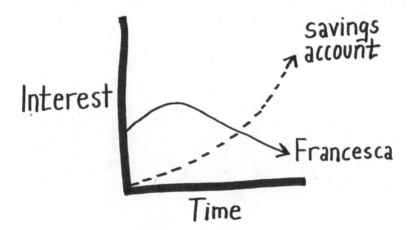

INVESTIGATION

Chapter 17

– – – ∼ – – – – – –

If I really want to find you on Facebook, no number of privacy settings is going to stop me.[7] So it was with Francesca Marcelo. It required a lot of searching and no finding, and then searching for her friends and friends of friends from high school, friending them, then scrolling through *their* friends for the *F*s. Eventually, I found her: Francesca Marcelo.

I messaged her about, you know, hanging out sometime while we were both home for Christmas. She was game. That's how I found myself standing on her porch on December 26, knocking on her front door and watching that stairway for her to come down, feeling much like I had a decade before when I'd come to pick her up for our golf course date. She appeared at the top of the stairway, and as she walked down I reviewed the script I had created in my

[7] Creepiest sentence in this book?

mind, the script for our conversation that would lead to all my questions being answered.

But here's the problem with scripts. They work great in movies. In life? Not so much. Life is too complicated. As soon as you involve other human beings and their unwieldy free wills, you can kiss your precious script good-bye.

She opened the door. Her hair was cut pixie short, and her clothes were even more earthy and hempy than they were back in high school. For a second I was not even sure it was her. But then I looked at those hazel eyes.

"Francesca Marcelo!" I said, smiling.

"Josh Sundquist!"

She wrapped her arms around my neck, and I put one forearm-crutch-attached hand around her waist while I kept my weight on the other crutch for balance.

"Come on in."

She led me downstairs to the basement to play a game of pool. I hoped, I wondered, if maybe she felt the same pent-up tension I did, the same lingering years-old interest that kept festering, kept saying *It's possible! We could be together! We should be together!*

I racked the balls and pushed them into the front of the triangle before lifting it away. I let her break. I didn't want to beat her too badly.

Francesca and I caught up on biographical information: college, graduation, current employment status, and the like. She asked me about my job as a motivational speaker. Bingo. That was the opening line in my script. She was following it perfectly.

"You remember back the first time we ever hung out," I began. "When my artificial leg malfunctioned on the golf course?"

She smiled. "Yeah, I remember."

"I actually tell that story in my speeches."

"About me?"

"Well, it's mostly about my leg, but yeah, it's about you, too."

I couldn't read her expression, couldn't determine whether she was pleased or dismayed with this revelation. I pressed forward, offering, "People really like it."

"That's good," she said noncommittally.

It was my turn in our game of pool, and I was lining up my shot. But I stood upright before taking it in order to pause the game while we proceeded into the dramatic climax of my script.

"In fact," I said, "people always come up to me after my speeches and say, 'What happened to you and Francesca?' And I'm never quite sure what to tell them." Here was the punch line. I looked straight across the pool table into her eyes to deliver it with maximum feeling. "What happened to us, Francesca?"

"I don't know," she said. "What *did* happen to us?"

I froze. This was not part of the script. She was supposed to answer the question, not deflect it back to me. I wanted her to tell me exactly what went wrong, why she didn't like me. Or to tell me that she did like me and for all these years, she'd been wishing our hanging out had turned into an actual relationship.

But instead of giving me an answer, she had turned the question around. That caught me off guard. I didn't have the answer. That's why I had asked *her*, after all.

I felt like we'd gone back in time ten years, returning to that golf course. I was falling in slow motion, down, down, down, landing on my back beside the tee, the foot of my artificial leg turned at an anatomically impossible angle. I looked up at her in shock and confusion and embarrassment, for a moment frozen there on the grass, unsure of what to say next. That's how I felt again, a decade later, in her basement. Caught in the headlights. She had asked me a question, but I was too scared to try to answer, almost like I knew exactly what had happened to us but was afraid to admit it to myself.

"Um, I don't know," I said.

She nodded slowly, almost sagely. And then she changed the subject, leaving me to wonder about that nod: Was she nodding to agree with the fact that I didn't know? As in, *You certainly* don't *know, do you? You still don't get it, and you probably never will.* Or was she nodding to show that she didn't know, either?

The nod was frustratingly ambiguous but the message clear: This was a question I would somehow have to answer for myself.

EVELYN
WILLIAMSON

BACKGROUND

Chapter 18

A neon-yellow indoor soccer ball whizzed past my head.

The ball hadn't been aimed at me, of course. Everyone could see I was standing on the sideline, deliberately sitting this one out, like I did most active games at youth group. Of course, it was my choice to wear my prosthesis. Without it, I could've hopped and participated. But I chose to wear it because the social aspect of youth group was more important than the dodgeball aspect, and I did better socially when I was wearing the leg. At least I had Evelyn to keep me company.

"Remember when you'd spend hours studying for the SATs every Saturday?" she asked, granting me the dignity of ignoring the near miss with the soccer ball. After all, she knew how it felt to be left out.

"Yeah. Every Saturday."

"Were you doing practice tests?"

"Sometimes. Or memorizing vocabulary flash cards."

She tucked an errant strand of brown hair behind her ear. She looked over at me with her manga-sized eyes and her curled eyelashes. She had a tall, thin, boxy frame, so our eyes met at the same height.

"Have you ever thought about doing something, you know, fun with your weekends?"

"First of all, that was last semester. I'm done with the SATs. Second of all, it *was* fun." It was spring semester, and I was back home after training in Colorado. I wasn't going to school, though, since I'd finished all my classes in December.

"Studying SAT words? Fun?"

"Yes, it was ubiquitous fun." After I said it I realized it was probably not the proper use of the word. Oh well.

"Seriously?"

"Yeah, I enjoy standardized tests."

"No, I mean did you seriously just use an SAT word to describe how much fun you were having while studying for the SATs?"

"I did. Thank you for noticing."

Joe Slater blew his whistle, and one of the dodgeball teams was declared victorious.

"You're so weird."

"Again, thank you."

"How many times did you end up taking the SATs?"

"Six."

Weirdness

number of times you take the SATs "for fun"

"That's a lot."

"Had fun every time."

"Now that you're done, maybe you should call me more often."

Ah. There it was. The point of this conversation.

"Maybe I will."

She smiled and poked me with her finger. "You should."

It annoyed me slightly when she flirted like this. Because, in fact, I was in love with her, or as close to love as you can be when you're seventeen and a member of the opposite sex has become your quasi best friend.

Evelyn's flirting always made me wonder: What if we were more than best friends? What would that be like? But as I said, it was slightly annoying, too. This was because of Mason, her on-again, off-again boyfriend.

"How are things with Mason?" I meant it partly as a reminder: *This is why I don't call you more often. You have a boyfriend.*

She sighed. "We're taking a break."

This sort of drama was nothing new. "You want to talk about it?"

Talking about her boyfriend was, of course, a total Friend Zone move. But that's exactly what she and I were: friends.

She looked down at her feet. The balls were flying again; another round had begun.

"He was home from college this weekend."

"Yeah?"

"But he said long distance was too hard."

"And he wanted to take a break?"

She nodded, her weight shifting on her closely watched feet.

"That sucks," I offered.

"Yeah. It sucks."

"How long has it been...since...how long have you been together?"

"This time?" She smirked and rolled her eyes. "Six months, I guess. But before that it was a year."

"That's a long time."

"He's right," she said. "I mean, it *is* hard. Long distance, I mean. It's really hard. But still..."

"But still," I echoed.

Like everyone in the history of the world who has had a crush on his or her best friend, I was too scared to tell her, because if I did I might lose her completely. And the sharp bite of losing her completely would be far worse than the one-sided romantic arrangement we had going.

Joe Slater blew a whistle, and the second game was over. We, the two disabled kids, joined the rest of the group.

I had a choice about whether I wanted to wear my leg or not. Evelyn, though, didn't have such a choice. Early in high school, she was a standout soccer star, a talented athlete with the gift of speed. But then she contracted early-onset rheumatoid arthritis, and now her joints moved too stiffly for soccer. I guess she could've played dodgeball tonight if she had wanted to, but her knees would swell up painfully for several days afterward. So instead the two of us stood and watched from the sidelines. It was something we had never explicitly discussed, this thing we shared. I guess it was both too obvious to warrant discussion and too painful to justify it.

Chapter 19

— — — — — — — — —

In April of what would have been my senior year, I was, unfortunately, nominated for prom king. How did this happen, since I wasn't even attending school and didn't exactly run with the cool crowd? I guess four years of saying hi to everyone in the hallway finally paid off.

Why do I say "unfortunately"? I mean, for a lot of students prom king or queen is the pinnacle of high school awesomeness, the greatest thing they could aspire to. But for me, not so much. Let me explain the way I looked at the situation. At my school four guys and four girls were nominated. Then there was a runoff vote with these eight nominees, and on prom night, before the dance started, they would all be called to the stage. One guy would be crowned prom king and one girl prom queen. And then the other six would walk off the stage in public humiliation, having just been declared not quite cool enough.

And since there were four male nominees, there was a 75 percent chance I would be one of the losers. Well, not really. Elections aren't determined by random probability. But since there were no preelection polls in the race for prom king, let's assume for the sake of discussion that my chances of winning were one in four. Which aren't great odds, obviously. I mean, even when I had cancer, my chances were fifty-fifty, and I recall being pretty worried about it at the time. And those odds were twice as high as my chances of winning prom king. So anyway, all this is why I considered my nomination to be unfortunate.

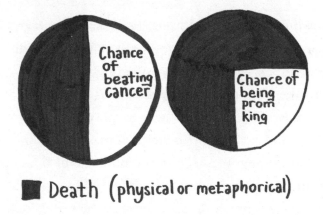

■ Death (physical or metaphorical)

On the other hand, there was always the outside chance I could win. And maybe the victory would catapult me into actually having fun at the dance. I could certainly use the boost. If there was one activity I felt insecure about as a result of having one leg, it was dancing.

My first school dance had been homecoming, which my parents finally allowed me to attend in tenth grade. I remember standing on the edge of the makeshift dance floor in the cafeteria. I wanted so desperately to join the other students, to dance with abandon, to have fun and be fun, to break out of my shell and break it down on my prosthesis. But I couldn't do it. My body, and especially my titanium-constructed left leg, was simply too stiff.

So in eleventh grade, I volunteered to serve punch at the homecoming dance. I wanted to be there for social reasons, but I needed a plausible excuse to hang out at the punch bowl all evening. It worked pretty well. But then came senior year and the unfortunate prom king nomination, which made it sort of impossible to skip the dance. And it would be tough to serve punch if I ended up being crowned the winner.

And this leads us to my most important problem: I had to find a date. Francesca already had one. Not that I would have had the guts to ask her anyway. And my go-to line— *We should hang out sometime*—wasn't as smooth when it came to finding a prom date.

A few nights later, I called Evelyn from the phone in my parents' bedroom.

"Hello?" It was her family's landline, but I recognized her voice.

"Hey, it's Josh. Do you re—"

"Yeah I remember you, silly. I'm on the other line with Mason."

"Oh, sorry. I can call back."

"No, it's fine—we were just about to hang up. Hold on."

The line went quiet for a moment. The fact that she had been talking to Mason suggested several things, none of them good.

"Josh?"

"Yup."

"Cool. What's up?"

"Not much. You?"

"Well, you know...just talking to Mason."

"How did that go?"

"He thinks he might have made a mistake by breaking up with me."

"Might have?"

"Yeah. But he's not sure yet."

"He's not sure?"

To me, it was obvious. Of course he had made a mistake. Who would ever dump Evelyn?

"Yeah, not sure."

"What would make him sure?"

"Well, I mean, obviously we love each other. But long distance is hard. You know?"

I didn't know, actually. I had never had a girlfriend, much less a long-distance one, much less known what it was like to truly be in love with someone who loved me, too. "Yeah. It sounds tough."

"I just don't know, Josh. I feel like Mason and I go through this cycle again and again and again. I just can't seem to stop."

I sat down on the bed. "Well, they say admitting you have a problem is the first step. So congrats on that."

"Thanks. What's the next step?"

Dating me, I thought.

"I'm not sure."

To be fair, Mason was a really cool guy. And I mean cool in a genuine sense, not cool as in popular. I knew him pretty well, and when I was honest with myself I had to admit that if I was a girl, I'd probably choose him over me, too. I just didn't understand why he wouldn't choose Evelyn in return.

I had this fantasy about Evelyn. But not the kind of fantasy you'd expect from a teenaged boy. My fantasy went like this: My girlfriend, Evelyn, would call me one afternoon, crying about a terrible fight she'd had with her mom or a devastating test score or something. In between sobs, she'd gasp out little sentences. She didn't know what to do. Her life was falling apart. Nothing made sense anymore.

"Hold on, babe," I'd say. "I'm coming for you."

I'd keep the pedal to the metal until I either arrived at her house or got pulled over.

"Son, do you know how fast you were going?" the cop would say.

I would set my jaw and look him squarely in the eye.

"With all due respect, sir," I would say. "Right now I think my girlfriend needs my warm embrace more than the Commonwealth of Virginia needs my money."

The cop would see from my heroic expression that the

only way to stop me would be to shoot me in the face. Then his hardened heart would melt in the light of my undying love.

"Follow me," he'd say.

He would get in his car and escort me with lights flashing and sirens blazing. We'd blow stop signs and traffic lights. When I got to Evelyn's driveway, I'd skid sideways, the back of my car whipping into her garage door and knocking it off its hinges so I could get inside faster. I'd run inside through the now-open garage and find her curled up in bed, crying. At the sight of me, she would jump into my arms.

"Shhhh, it's okay. I'm here now," I'd say.

And I would know from the tightness of her grip around my chest how much she needed me, and how the strength of my embrace was restoring her sense of well-being. She would feel better. I would feel needed.

"So how are you?" Evelyn asked.

"I'm good. Yeah, really good. . . . Guess what?"

"What?"

"Guess."

"Okay . . ." she said. "You made the US ski team?"

"Um, no, few years away from that."

Now that I was home from Colorado, I still went to school functions (sporting events, senior proms, etc.) but wasn't at school every day, so I didn't have access to the up-to-the-minute stats about who had a date and who didn't. That's partially why Evelyn was a good choice to be my date. She was from another school. I knew she was available. That, and the fact that she was superhot. And she was my best friend. If there was anyone I could let loose with and have fun with on the dance floor, it would be her.

"Guess again."

"I give up."

"Okay. You ready for this?"

"I don't know. Am I?"

"I was nominated for prom king."

"Wow, really?"

"Yeah!"

"Josh, that's awesome. Congrats."

"Thanks."

"But you hate dances."

"I know."

"What are you going to do?"

"Find a date, I guess," I replied.

She chuckled.

"As a matter of fact," I willed myself to press on, "I was wondering if you might possibly want to go with me?"

There was a horrendously long pause that lasted at least one full second.

Finally, she said, "I would love to."

I hoped she couldn't hear my sigh of relief. "Great. It will be fun."

"I think so, too. I've never gone to a dance with a prom king," she said.

"Neither have I."

She laughed. "Maybe it will be a first for both of us, then."

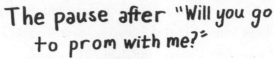

The pause after "Will you go to prom with me?"

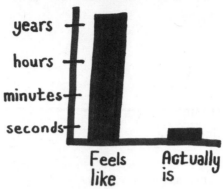

"Maybe. But realistically, I probably won't win. I mean, I don't want to get your hopes up."

"Of course you'll win, Josh Sundquist. But I'll go to prom with you either way."

"Thanks. I appreciate your commitment."

I gave her the details. A few of her friends from Spotswood High had boyfriends at Harrisonburg High. She suggested we could get dinner with them before the dance. I had already thought of this, but I acted like I hadn't and agreed it was a stellar idea.

"Call me again soon," she said.

"I will," I promised.

"I appreciate your commitment," she said.

I smiled. "Bye."

"See you."

Chapter 20

- - - - - - - - -

At dinner the next Monday, Dad revealed the complex prom compensation package he and Mom had devised in response to my pleas for financial assistance.

"We will pay for the tickets to the dance," he said. "And half of dinner. You're on your own for the tuxedo rental."

I knew this last part was a concession to my mom, who bought all her clothes at thrift stores. She would think that I should just buy a black suit and bow tie from Goodwill rather than rent a tux.

"What about After Prom?" I asked. After Prom was the accurately but not creatively titled event that took place following the dance. It was basically a big G-rated party hosted by the parents where students could participate in quasi-fun activities that did not involve alcohol or pregnancy.

"What about it?" asked Dad.

"You're not going to pay for my tickets? They're only ten dollars each."

"We believe you can afford that," said Dad.

"You know," I said, lowering my voice slightly to convey gravity, "studies show that if a couple does not attend After Prom, the girl is far more likely to end up getting—"

"Okay, okay, all right," he interrupted. Luke and Anna were both pre-birds-and-bees talk, and Dad didn't want me saying the p-word around them, which could lead to uncomfortable dinner-table questions about the mechanics of reproduction. "We'll pay for your After Prom tickets."

"In that case, I guess I can get by without getting a job."

Mom let out a sigh of relief.

"If..." said Dad.

"Here it comes," I said.

"You do the dishes tonight."

I smiled. "Deal. Nice doing business with you."

The next afternoon I went to rent my tuxedo. I wasn't quite as frugal as my mom—that is, I didn't want to buy a tuxedo from the seventies at a thrift store—but neither did I want to drop three figures on a rental from an upscale tuxedo shop. I knew just the place to go, a super-sad-looking wedding supply store in the first floor of a two-story house near my high school. The living room window had been converted into a display case featuring a creepy mannequin (is there any other kind?) in a bridal gown, and a sign that read TUXEDO RENTAL $30. I knew a good deal when I saw one.

"I'd like one of those thirty-dollar tuxedos, please."

"Do you want the shoes, too?"

"Do they come with it?"

"No, they're twenty extra."

I owned a pair of shoes. In fact, I owned several pairs of shoes. So I decided that there was no reason to spend an extra twenty dollars. After all, I was here to rent a *tuxedo*. That's the piece I didn't own.

"No, thanks. Just the tux."

They had two sizes remaining. I chose the one that fit less worse.

When I got home, Mom asked if I had ordered the corsage yet.

"What is a corsage again?" I asked.

"The flowers. These days it's usually on an elastic band that goes around the girl's wrist."

"Hmm...is it important?"

"Yes."

"Well, no, I haven't."

"I called around to the flower shops for you," she said. "I found one that has them for only six dollars."

"Oh, thanks. That sounds like a good deal."

"Yes, and, well," she said, as if she had something stuck in her throat, "I would like to buy it for you. If you want."

She smiled a smile that revealed both her pain in offering to pay six dollars and her pleasure in giving me a gift that would enhance my chances with Evelyn.

"Thanks, Mom," I said, hugging her.

"You're welcome. Do you know what color Evelyn's dress is?"

"No. Why?"

"I need to tell the flower shop."

"Why do they care?"

"So they can match the flowers with her dress."

"Really?"

"Yes, really."

"People care about that stuff?"

"*Girls* care about that stuff."

I slept until three thirty on the day of prom in order to be well rested for staying up all night. Unfortunately, this also meant I started the day behind schedule. I scrambled to take a shower, shave, and put on my tux. That last part turned out to be incredibly complicated, involving a highly inefficient and antiquated buttoning system down the front and French cuffs that required cuff links, which are virtually impossible to put on if you have the unfortunate disadvantage of being born with only two hands. The only easy part was the bow tie, because it was of the pre-tied, clip-on variety. Anyway, I was supposed to pick up Evelyn for dinner at four thirty, and I left approximately on time, but after driving a few miles it hit me: I had forgotten the corsage.

I wheeled around and drove back to my house, where my mom retrieved the corsage from the refrigerator. By the time I left again, it was already four thirty, and I still had at least a fifteen-minute drive to Evelyn's house. I was sweating profusely and breathing short, shallow breaths. This was such an important night and here I was ruining it because I was late. I drove eighty-five in a fifty-five, faster than I ever had before, on my way to her house. It was kind of like my fantasy about her, except instead of speeding heroically so I could comfort her sooner, I was driving frantically because I was having a mild panic attack.

I skidded to a stop in front of her house and hobbled on my artificial leg up to the front porch. She answered on the first knock, literally right after my fist made contact with

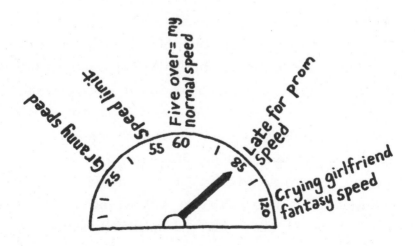

the door, so when my hand returned for a second knuckle-rap the door was already opening and I nearly punched Evelyn with a palm-forward fist.

"Are you okay?" she asked.

"Yeah, why?" I said, breathing heavily.

"You look...sweaty."

This isn't really what anyone, guy or girl, wants to hear upon being inspected in their formal attire by their prom date.

"It's really hot out."

"Is it?" She extended her arm outside to feel the temperature. "Yeah. I guess."

"I'm so sorry I'm late."

"No problem."

I looked at her for the first time. When you make your initial examination of the appearance of your female prom date, you must balance the competing obligation (and desire) to linger over the curves of her body long enough to appreciate the thought and care that went into her dress selection with the fact that her father is standing in the foyer immediately behind her, and he is looking at you looking at his daughter. I started with her feet, which were adorned casually in flip-flops—a nice choice, especially given the exceedingly non-prom-like wing tips I was wearing—that matched the color of her dress. The dress was a long silver gown with a thin mesh netting over a base of silk. It started at her ankles and ended below her shoulders. Her hair was glued and glittered like some kind of complex decorative piece of pottery that would shatter if it was dropped.

She looked beautiful. But I didn't want to just say that: *Hi there, you look beautiful.* Because that was what I was expected to say. That's what all gentlemen say to their prom dates. Mom had taught me that. Even if she hadn't looked beautiful, I would have said it anyway. It was the appropriate remark for the occasion. Precisely because it was so appropriate, so perfunctory, however, I wanted to say something more so she would know she really did look absolutely beautiful, so she would know I noticed the way the elegantly shimmering dress matched her nails and the way it all radiated out from her big brown eyes like rays from the sun. But again, her dad was standing right there.

"You look beautiful," I said, adding a slight but meaningful pause in between the second and third words.

"Thank you." She beamed. "And you look very handsome."

Which I didn't, I knew. I looked very sweaty. But it was the polite thing to say, and Evelyn was a polite girl.

She invited me in for the exchange of wearable flower arrangements, a ceremony her mother was already poised to photograph with paparazzi-like eagerness. I unwrapped the six-dollar corsage my mom had given me. It was blue and white. I slipped it over Evelyn's wrist, the flashbulb strobe-lighting the room. Evelyn's mother produced a boutonniere and handed it to her. Evelyn removed the pin from the stem and stepped so close I could taste her perfume on my tongue.

"I'll try not to stick you," she said. Similar to *You look beautiful*, this is the obligatory line uttered by every human being who has ever installed a pin-attached flower arrangement to the lapel of another human being. It's not funny—particularly if yours is the epidermis in question—but you have to laugh anyway.

We posed for a variety of other photos and then we were off.

I put a mix CD that did not include any of Ani DiFranco's work in the car stereo.

By way of making conversation, I said, "Have you decided about college yet?"

She shook her head. "No. I was pretty set on Virginia Tech, but now with Mason and me being...on a break... I'm not so sure."

"Whaddaya mean?"

"Like, maybe I just wanted to go there to be with him."

I nodded. "Well, better to find that out now than go there, break up freshman year, and realize you had just followed him to school." I wondered whether my words revealed too much glee over her partial singleness.

"At the same time," she added, "I don't want to *not* go there just because he's there. I mean, maybe that's the best college for me, you know? I can't plan my entire life around avoiding him."

"True, true. No one likes a reverse stalker." I wished silently that she had applied to William and Mary.

"Do you think you'll get back together?" I asked.

"No. I mean, yeah, probably. I don't know."

We were silent for a while, thinking. I knew they most likely would get back together eventually. I mean, historically speaking, a definite pattern had emerged: So far, 100 percent of their previous breakups had resulted in passionate reunions, in getting-back-together-agains. And as they say, history repeats itself.

But right now, tonight, she was more or less single. If ever I had a chance, this was it. It all seemed to hang on whether I won prom king. If I won, maybe that would give me the confidence boost I needed to be a fun dancing partner, and then to try to kiss her or tell her how I felt. And maybe it would help her think of me as more than a friend. If I was prom king, I might become, in her eyes, something more.

On the other hand, maybe she'd just be happy that her good friend Josh Sundquist had won a popularity contest. Maybe she thought of me like a brother or maybe she valued our friendship too much to see if there was something more there. That was the problem. Back when I had been trying to date Francesca, the issue had been that I didn't have a friend to help me understand the relationship. The problem with Evelyn? She *was* the friend.

It all came down to tonight.

Chapter 21

Obviously, you want to go somewhere fancy to eat on the night of prom, which is why our group chose one of the classiest joints in Harrisonburg, an upscale seafood establishment called Red Lobster.

There were six of us, three couples. After dinner, we went to one of the guys' houses for more photos. Prom is nothing more than a practice round, a dress rehearsal for your wedding, and in no arena is this fact on more prominent display than the number of photos taken leading up to the event. Sometimes you get the feeling that the photos are more important than the event itself.

On the drive from the photo session to the school, Evelyn asked, "Do you think you'll win prom king?"

"Honestly? Not really."

Well, I thought I had as good a chance as the other three guys. And I wanted to win. Mainly to impress Evelyn, to sweep her off her feet with my popularity and esteem in the eyes of my fellow students. But relationships are all about managing expectations, you know?

"I think you'll win," she stated.

"How come?"

"Because you're Josh Sundquist."

"That is my name, yes."

"And Josh Sundquist is a winner."

I wasn't so sure. But I said, "Thanks for saying that."

"Seriously. You're going to win."

She reached over and grabbed my hand, squeezed, and released. It felt tingly and amazing. It felt like I was enough for her, like she liked me, like everyone in my class liked me and had voted for me. It felt like I was prom king.

"I hope you're right," I said.

Once we finally got to the dance, we were forced to endure for the sake of the parents and their all-important photographs a long, boring ritual known as "introductions." The introductions ceremony would conclude with the naming of the prom king and queen, which was great because it meant if I lost, not only would all my classmates know, all their parents would find out, too. A crowd of nearly one thousand would be on hand to witness my humiliation.

After you were introduced with your date, the two of you had to walk down a portable staircase in front of center stage. It is exceedingly difficult to walk on stairs with a hip-disartic-level prosthesis without a handrail, as was the case here. To make matters worse, Evelyn would have her arm hooked around my elbow, so her descent could easily knock me off balance.

As I stood there in line, awaiting our turn, I thought of this experience I'd had when I was a freshman. I was still fresh off the boat from homeschooling, nervous about navigating the halls of the school on my artificial leg.

One day, as I was about to head down a flight of stairs, this upperclassman I sort of knew from one of my classes walked up beside me. She was flirty and pretty. I remember she seemed so much older. As I took my first step down the stairs, she hooked her hand through my left elbow as if I was escorting her somewhere, and said, "Let's go, darling!"

In an instant, I felt like I had grown five inches taller. Here I was, a lowly freshman and former homeschooler, and this attractive senior girl had seen fit to bestow her attention upon me. Not only that, but *our bodies were touching.* She had looked at me and thought, Hey, I'd like to grab that boy's arm and hold on to it. She wanted to be seen walking down the stairs with me, arm in arm. It was like a dream, that moment.

In the next instant, however, I foresaw how poorly this would turn out. Obviously, she had never seen me walk down stairs, which I managed by holding on to the handrail with one hand and gripping my books under my arm with the other. I would then bend my right knee, descending first with my artificial foot, which would land stiff-legged two steps below and support my body weight while I brought the real foot down beside it. I would repeat this process, two steps at a time, stepping all the way down the staircase. Anyway, it worked all right as a means of descent, but it was not smooth enough for me to keep my balance while a pretty girl held on to one of my arms.

But as we started to walk down the stairs together, I was too mortified to say anything. She had made this wonderfully kind and ego-inflating gesture, and as her reward she was going to trip the disabled guy. She held on for the first awkward step as I placed my artificial leg two levels down. Then I lowered the rest of my body to that stair in one quick motion, jerking hers along with me. She ripped her hand back like my arm had turned into a hot stove. We walked the rest of the way down in silence. I kept my gaze on the stairs, focusing on keeping my balance. We parted without a word at the base of the stairs, and after that we never spoke again. I don't mean to make it sound like she was a jerk. The feeling was mutual. Shame. Shame and embarrassment on my part; shame and guilt on hers. That moment in the stairwell may have set a world record for the shortest romantic relationship of all time. And after our breakup, there was just too much baggage between us to be able to acknowledge each other anymore.

I could not let that happen to Evelyn and me. I would walk down smoothly and most importantly, I would not fall.

As I neared the front of the line, I forgot all about the prom king race. My fear was concentrated on those six steps.

I was next. As I limped across the stage, into the bright lights, I heard the vice principal read our names. Evelyn made it to the center a moment before I did and waited for me. We joined arms, her forearm linked under my left elbow. The audience applauded politely.

We strode to the front of the stage and I stopped where it ended, dropping off into the dark abyss that was the portable staircase. The auditorium went silent while the vice principal waited for us to clear the stage so he could read the next pair of names. Someone coughed. I wished that we had practiced this ahead of time, or at least discussed it. I could've given her some pointers, lowered her expectations a bit. Or suggested we forgo the arm holding altogether, which would have made it easier for me to balance. But I couldn't very well let go of her arm now, not with all these people watching and her being unprepared for it. I made a single tentative movement, placing the heel of my artificial leg on the top step. The steps were narrow, not wide enough to fit the length of an entire foot, artificial or otherwise. Thus I had to balance solely on the heel of my prosthetic foot. As I moved the rest of my body down to that level, Evelyn stepped with me, then paused while I planted my prosthesis on the second step. Once my balance was set, we moved down together. The spotlights onstage still lit up our faces, but our feet and knees were enshrouded in darkness. Without a handrail, the middle steps of a six-step staircase are the scariest section, because you have departed the safe nest of the wide, flat stage, but you aren't yet in the warm embrace of the auditorium floor, either. In other words, if you lose your balance, you're going for a tumble.

But I was careful. And Evelyn never retracted her hand, even when it was clear that I was having great difficulty, even though a thousand people were watching us struggle. She held on through all of it, until the next names had been called and we were finding our seats in the mercifully anonymous darkness.

Unfortunately, it wasn't long until I heard Vice Principal Harry Maguire say, "Would the following nominees come to the stage...."

I felt a shot of adrenaline. Evelyn whispered in my ear, "Good luck."

When Mr. Maguire got to my name, I walked down the center aisle, but instead of going up that precariously handrail-less stairway in the middle, I veered to the left so I could use the one on the wing, which had a nice, stable rail bolted into the brick wall. I listened to the way the audience clapped after my name. Were they clapping louder for me than for the other three guys, all of whose names had already been called? I told myself that they were.

The four of us lined up in alphabetical order—Trevor Binot, Joseph Chuk, Jon Heinrich, and me. These three guys were not only on the football team, they *were* the football team. In other words, they were the guys you'd expect to be on this stage right now. They were the popular guys, the ones with cars from this decade.

"Ladies and gentlemen, your prom court!" Mr. Maguire said after the girls were onstage, too.

Then, two girls came out from backstage, each holding a crown sitting on top of a red satin pillow. The girls were both freshmen, and they were dressed in almost-matching gowns. They reminded me of the flower girls at a wedding.

I glanced once more at my three competitors. It occurred to me that perhaps it wasn't so bad that they were more popular than me. In fact, that they all ran in the same social circles could be to my advantage. The three of them would, in effect, split the "popular" vote. And that would leave me as the only possible candidate for everyone else to vote for. I was the nominee of the commoners, the voice of the people. All those cynics who hated the popular crowd, all those who were disengaged from the social politics of high school but whose name I had always remembered when we passed in the hall, all those would be my votes!

"And this year's prom king is . . ."

I was the populist hero of the huddled masses! The forgotten majority, the underappreciated poor in spirit and the less than popular, they would flock to me! They would vote for me! I would be their king!

"Joseph Chuk!"

The audience burst into applause. I numbly followed suit. With regal grace, Joseph inclined his head so the flower girl could place upon it the majestic crown, bejeweled as it was with hard plastic gemstones. That was *my* crown. I was supposed to be the one wearing it. Joe waved to the crowd, acknowledging the adoration of his faithful subjects. I was supposed to win prom king, to have the confidence to dance, to confess my feelings to Evelyn. This was my prom. It was supposed to be perfect. For me.

As I walked back up the aisle to sit beside Evelyn, I didn't make eye contact with anyone in the audience. These people had seen me lose. They had chosen not to vote for me, and now they sat there all smug, watching my walk of shame.

"Don't worry about it," Evelyn whispered as I sat back down. "It's just a stupid popularity contest."

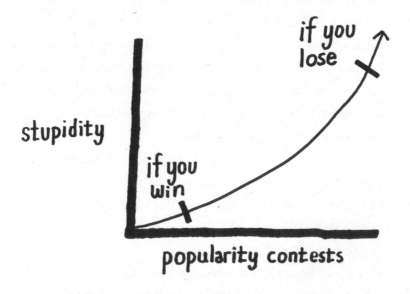

Chapter 22

— — — — — — — — —

The night was already over. It was a nonstarter, a failure to launch. I might as well drive home right now, I thought. But I couldn't abandon Evelyn. She held on to me when we walked down those stairs. I could stick with her for one night of shame and humiliation.

We walked into the open section of the cafeteria that had been converted into a dance floor for prom. There were a lot of decorations, and it was clear that substantial thought and time had gone into making sure they fit together as part of some overall theme. It was hard to say what the theme was, exactly, but it apparently had something to do with fairy tales, castles, and large cardboard stars with glitter on them. The room was already packed with several hundred people, and on one side the DJ had set up shop with several towers of speakers, blinking lights, and, yes, a disco ball.

I was pleased to find the DJ had just started a slow

dance. Fast dances are hard. There is a lot of moving, and all this moving requires either skill, the ability to fake skill, or the ability to not care what people think about your lack of skill. I lacked all these traits. Slow dances, on the other hand, were simple. You just put your hands on the girl's waist and then spun around in circles until the music stopped. No skill required.

That said, slow dances tend to be hard in, shall we say, another area. It's no secret that girls usually find it weird or even gross when they feel this activity in a boy's body while dancing with him. And as a teenaged guy, this is frustrating. Because it's not as if we have a choice in the matter. But there are things you can do. Like math. While we spun in our slow, tight circle, I did multiplication tables in my head. Six times seven is forty-two. Six times eight is forty-eight. Six times nine... anything to keep my mind off the fact that my body was in very, very close proximity to that of a female.

When you see teenaged couples slow dancing, usually you'll notice that the boy is holding the girl at arm's length, keeping an awkward distance between them. Girls often assume this is because the boy feels uncomfortable or self-conscious about dancing. Maybe. But I would suggest that if you look more closely, you may discover it's not the dancing he feels self-conscious about.

Anyway, eventually the song ended and people clapped as they always weirdly do at the end of slow-dance songs, as if applauding their own ability to stand in one place and spin around for three minutes without getting dizzy. The music veered to hip-hop, which meant fast dancing. Evelyn and I took a step back from each other, and then I took another one, so we were starting to blend into the circle of acquaintances that occupied this region of the dance floor. Then I started to dance. I transferred my weight back and forth between real and fake leg, simultaneously making a motion with my arms like I was pedaling a hand-powered bicycle. Pretty hip. Soon enough the group became an actual circle, like we were playing a standing version of ring-around-the-rosy. Except we weren't. Instead, we were just making awkward eye contact with each other while pretending we were having a good time pretending we felt comfortable dancing.

That's normal fast dancing for you. Everyone stands around and tries to let the music infect them like a virus, one whose primary symptom is rhythmic convulsions and muscle spasms. There's another kind of fast dancing, though—what I refer to as Close Fast Dancing, or CFD.

CFD, unlike its more lustful and notorious cousin grinding, is more fun than sexual. It's basically where a couple assumes a slow-dance position but sways and spins at the speed of a fast dance. It's like ballroom dancing minus the skill, elegance, and rhythm. Sometimes people say grinding when they mean CFD, because said people have not seen what grinding really looks like. How can you tell the difference? It's in the name, people. When you see a couple grinding, there is simply no other word to describe it. They are *grinding*. When you see a couple holding each other and bouncing back and forth, probably smiling, they are engaging in CFD. The other way to tell the difference is in the axis or plane of motion. When grinding, a couple is moving their hips toward and away from each other, a forward-and-backward squeezing motion on the y-axis. When CFDing, by contrast, a couple is moving their hips left and right, a side-to-side swinging motion on the x-axis. Got it?

Anyway, CFDing still requires a degree of confidence, because you must intentionally put your arms around her waist. There is no question about whether she reciprocates. She either starts dancing with you, or shrinks away and slips into a protective enclave of her girlfriends, who will then form an impenetrable circular fortress around her and give you mean looks until you back off. So the risk of public rejection is very high.

Evelyn and I danced in the open circle for a few songs, me thinking the whole time how I should try to CFD with her. Suddenly she started walking across the circle toward me. Had she been having the same thought? Was she coming to CFD with me?

She grabbed my shoulders and pulled me toward her. This is it, I thought. We are going to do it. "I need to rest," she said in my ear.

Oh yeah. Arthritis. I nodded my understanding. Then

I wondered: Am I supposed to accompany her? Is that what a prom date does? I wasn't sure. So I asked.

"Do you want me to go with you?"

"No, Rachel is coming."

Was I still supposed to go with her? I wasn't sure. But having a disability of my own, I knew there was nothing more cringe-inducing than the feeling that someone else is giving up an activity you can't do just so you don't feel left out. A disability is already such a burden on you personally. It only gets worse when it's a burden on other people, too.

"All right, I'll just keep dancing. Come back out when you're ready," I said.

Truthfully, I was looking for an excuse to stop dancing. I didn't much enjoy it. But I had talked myself out of following Evelyn for fear she was trying to get away from me.

She made a face I couldn't read.

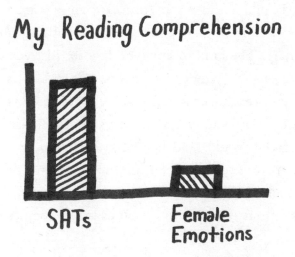

My Reading Comprehension

SATs

Female
Emotions

She nodded at her friend and the two of them peeled off from the circle and headed for the snack area, where there were cafeteria tables covered with red paper tablecloths. The tables were overflowing with shiny confetti that was getting tracked back to the dance floor on the smooth leather soles of dress shoes.

I danced, then, by myself in the circle of acquaintances. I felt uncoordinated and self-conscious, like everyone was looking at me and laughing inside. Since my prosthesis was attached at the hip, I was essentially sitting on it with the bones of my pelvis, the socket synched around my waist like a plaster corset. The leg itself, with its three stiff titanium and aluminum joints, was engineered for stability, not for getting down. I felt like I was trying to dance while tied in a seated position to a cement block.

I wondered if perhaps prom could still be salvaged. Maybe I could summon some dormant courage and become a fun dancer, the kind of guy who CFDs with his gorgeous prom date. The kind of guy who ignores his recent electoral defeat, who ignores his peers who did not vote for him and instead focuses on Evelyn. And if I could do that, maybe later we would sit at one of those confetti-sprinkled tables and I would hold her hand and wonder aloud if maybe there wasn't something more than friendship between us.

The circle collapsed on itself as a few couples paired

off to CFD. A few songs later the DJ brought it back to the old school (his words, not mine) with some early-nineties hip-hop. A much larger circle opened up in the center of the room as a guy named Jerome spun around on the floor, pivoting over his hands, swinging his lower body in gymnast-like ways. I felt a poke in my side. It was Evelyn. She smiled at me. People started chanting Jerome's name, *Jaa-ROME, Jaa-ROME, Jaa-ROME,* and he brought the spectacle to a climactic finale, freezing in a handstand and then scissoring his legs into a brief spin on his head.

Jerome bowed and people applauded like the best slow dance ever had just concluded. There was an expectant pause. The empty circle held its space while everyone hoped that someone else, that is, another person besides themselves, would jump into the middle and provide additional entertainment.

Eventually someone did.

Me.

Chapter 23

– – – – – – – – – –

My artificial leg had three joints: ankle, knee, and hip. That's one reason why it's tough to walk with a hip-disarticulation prosthesis, and why so few amputees who lose their leg at that level (that is, amputees who have no residual limb, or stump) choose to wear a fake leg. Let me break it down for you: My ankle didn't move the way a normal ankle would. It was only capable of rotation, not flexion. Like the motion you would need for a golf swing. My knee moved more like a real one in the sense that it could swing on the plane of motion you would expect from a human knee. To take a step, I would place the fake leg in front of me and then roll across the foot, the knee being designed to bend when my weight hit the toes. This weight-induced bend in the knee would store energy in a pressurized hydraulic piston, which would then push back like a spring, propelling the knee back to a straight position and swinging the prosthesis into a forward step. That's how I walked.

There was also my hip joint, which I typically engaged only to move into a sitting position. But the hip joint also provided my favorite feature of the prosthesis, which was its ability to extend far beyond the range of a normal human hip. Translation: I could easily do a split. Even better, I could do a split while standing up. I would balance on my real leg, lifting my artificial one with my hand and pulling it straight up until the foot pointed backward behind my head.

It was this particular party trick I employed in the dance cipher.[8] I jumped into the middle, picking my prosthesis up by the ankle and hopping in a tight spin, waving the fake foot in between two positions, one where I held the straight leg out in front of me, the foot at eye level, and one where it was fully extended in an unnatural standing split with the heel touching my ear. It was no secret that I was an amputee, which I suppose was fortunate because otherwise this would have looked supercreepy, like I was some kind of manic yogi-ballerina. As it was, everyone was in on the joke, and as I hopped around the circle, they cheered and, yes, even chanted my name. For the record, they had not chanted Joseph Chuk's name when he was crowned prom king. Take that, popularity contests.

Obviously, there could not have been a better moment to try to CFD with Evelyn.

---

[8] "Cipher" being the technical name for a circle of spectators formed around a break-dancer. Good to know, right?

The circle closed and I danced my way over to Evelyn. I got really close to her, but I stood so our bodies were facing each other at a ninety-degree angle. I figured this would feel less threatening to her than approaching her from straight on. Oh, she would think, Josh is standing really close to me, but our bodies are facing perpendicular directions, so I guess I am comfortable with this.

She glanced at my face and I smiled at her. She smiled back. I kept hand-cycling. Then she rotated her body away from me and took a small but discernible step to create space between us. Classic fast-dancing conundrum: Was she trying to get away from me, or had her attention been drawn to the sparkly disco ball?

So I danced the rest of that song wondering about this.

"Are you having fun?" she asked.

"Yeah!" I said, which was sort of a lie. I mean, I wasn't *not* having fun. So maybe there was some fun here that I was having without noticing, and I would look back later and think how fun it was, in retrospect. The past has a way of turning up the fun volume in your memories.

"Great." She put a hand on my shoulder, and for the briefest instant I thought we were about to CFD. "I gotta tell Rachel something."

This was twice now that she had put me off. Was she doing it on purpose? I couldn't be sure. I wanted to just give up, to quit trying to CFD with her, and spend the rest

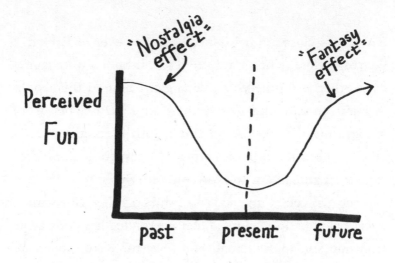

Perceived Fun

"Nostalgia effect"   "Fantasy effect"

past   present   future

of the night floating around, not caring. But that was the problem: I *did* care. I cared a lot. About her. About *us*. And we were both going to college in just a few months, and after that I wouldn't be seeing much of her. So what did I have to lose (I mean, besides my pride and dignity)? Tonight was probably my last chance with Evelyn. Who knew when she would get back together with Mason, when she would disappear completely from my life? Yes, tonight. Tonight was the night.

So I followed her over to her gossip session with Rachel, and when she leaned away and smiled at me, I leaned in and—yes, must reach out, almost there, just a little farther— put a hand ever so gently on her hip. "Hey," I said.

She smiled and made a quick glance down at my hand. It was very brief, and I supposed she hoped I didn't see it.

But I did. What I couldn't see, unfortunately, was how she felt about it.

"Hey," she answered.

I started to sort of bop back and forth like people do when they are dancing. She smiled a tight, toothless smile.

She held up a finger. "Hold on. Just a second. I'll be right back."

My hand was left holding air as her body rotated away from me so she could return her mouth to Rachel's ear. I saw Rachel steal a brief look at me and nod. Were they talking about me? Was Evelyn telling her she wanted to get away from me, that she was uncomfortable with my advances? Yes, probably. This was a mistake. All of it. Prom. Dancing. Evelyn. All a giant, soul-crushing mistake.

This guy Alberto who I knew, and who I guess knew Evelyn somehow, came up from behind her and started grinding on her. She took a quick look over her shoulder to see who it was. Upon seeing Alberto, she burst out laughing, like he was the funniest guy she'd ever seen, and what a hilarious joke this was that he was dancing with her like this. She pumped her hands in the air, raising the roof, smiling. He put a hand on her hip. She laughed again.

If Evelyn had been my girlfriend, I would've said something witty and manly to Alberto, you know, like, *Get your own date*, and then clocked him in the jaw. But Evelyn wasn't my girlfriend, so her heart was not mine to defend. The song ended, and Alberto hugged her and then walked away, in search of some other guy whose night he could ruin by dancing with his date.

I didn't recover after that. In terms of trying to CFD with Evelyn, I mean. I had tried three times, which was more than enough.

She didn't care about me. Our friendship? What a joke. We weren't friends. She was just a hot girl I had a crush on. Would I have been friends with her if I didn't have that crush? Probably not. Would she have been friends with me? Again, probably not. She was just using me for the attention. She had that female intuition or whatever that told her I liked her, and she was keeping me around because it felt good to have a boy pining for her, bringing her to his prom and listening to her talk about her boy problems. What a mistake all this had been. What a joke.

After the dance, we went to After Prom, which was held in the recreation center at James Madison University. Everyone brought duffel bags with normal clothes and changed out of their formal wear in the locker rooms. Evelyn was tired, and her knees hurt. She mostly sat with Rachel, both of them in their sweats, both of them encouraging their dates to go have fun, don't worry about us. So that's what I did. I had fun. Or at least I tried to. I sang karaoke and I played poker with Monopoly money. I jumped in a big inflatable thing. I drank tons of soda.

The After Prom party went till nearly sunrise. Then we all went over to this guy Jon's house. His mom had a breakfast spread for us. We ate and went to the basement to watch a movie. Evelyn found a guest room and went to sleep. When people started leaving, I woke her up and drove her home.

"I had fun," she said when I was dropping her off.

"Yeah," I said. "Thanks for coming."

I did not say I had fun. Because I hadn't, not really.

I didn't call Evelyn much after that. I graduated. Summer came. It got hot. Then it was fall, and we both went off to be college students. She ended up not going to the same school as Mason. But she was dating him again. Or so I had heard.

HYPOTHESIS

Based on subject's lack of interest in enacting the cultural mating ritual of Close Fast Dancing, I assume she did not have romantic interest in me. Further investigation is required to determine why subject demonstrated perplexing emotional distance at prom despite deep platonic friendship.

INVESTIGATION

Chapter 24

- - - - - - - - -

Evelyn looked exactly the same as she did in high school. We were having lunch at a sandwich place in Harrisonburg a few days after Christmas. Lunch, because it is the most decidedly unromantic, non-date-like social encounter two people can have. And all this because, well, Evelyn was now married. To that on-again, off-again boyfriend she'd had during high school, Mason. I guess they'd worked everything out and decided to stay on-again forever. Anyway, I had not seen her in years. But as I said, she looked the same.

Which is not to say things *felt* the same. When you have a crush on someone who has a boyfriend, it's a little weird; you convince yourself she may come to her senses and start dating you instead. Even engaged people have been known (in movies) to make a game-time decision to leave the altar and run away with the Person They Were Supposed to Be With.

Real Weddings

■ Someone objects
□ Audience forever holds its peace

In Movies

But once that girl you had a crush on is *married*, it's time to admit defeat. She chose. Forever. Without you.

So the dynamic was different between Evelyn and me. There was a palpable gap between us, a gravity that kept pulling us back toward the emotional safe ground of small talk. But I knew I had to push through. I had come to this lunch to figure out why it didn't work out between us, and why after we had been best friends for so long she was so disappointingly distant at prom, and I was not going to let the sanctity of marriage stop me from getting my answers. I saw my opportunity at one point while we were reminiscing about old times.

"Remember when we went to prom together?" I tried

to say it like, *Ha-ha, wasn't that funny like these other funny things we've been talking about,* but there was still a shift in my tone. Her face said she noticed it.

"Yeah. Senior year?"

I nodded. "That was fun."

"A lot of fun."

I bit my lip. "But..."

"What?"

"I don't know. I just felt like things were kind of awkward that night." I paused, choosing my words carefully. "Like you were sort of... like it just felt weird."

"Yeah, you're right. That was because I had such a big crush on you," she said, taking a casual sip of her water.

If I had been taking a sip of my own water in that moment, I'm sure I would've spit it all over the table, *phhhhh*ing it out at high pressure in all directions.

"Um, what?" I had heard her the first time. But there was no way. I must have misunderstood.

"I said, that was because I had such a big crush on you."

"You did?" I was still in disbelief.

"Um, yeah," she said, like she was saying *duh.*

"You had a crush on me?"

"Of course."

"No, not of course. You always had a boyfriend."

"Not always," she said. "Anyway, you really didn't know I liked you?"

"Um, no."

She shrugged. "I always thought you knew."

"Nope."

"Well...surprise!" She shrugged again. She was married. She had found her Prince Charming. This was old news to her.

"So why didn't you want to dance with me at prom?"

"I was nervous around you. That kind of thing."

I shook my head. I had been so worried about winning prom king to impress her. So she would like me. But she already did like me. The whole time, from the beginning.

"I'm sorry, this is just kind of crazy to hear," I said.

"It's funny that you never knew."

"Yeah, hilarious," I said sarcastically.

"Not ha-ha funny, just interesting funny," she said. "I mean, I always used to wonder, you know, what it would be like. If we were together."

"Why didn't you tell me?"

"I did."

"False."

"Well, I always asked you to call me."

"And you asked your boyfriend to *date* you. Seriously, you guys were together most of high school."

"Sometimes we were broken up. And those were the times."

"The times what?"

"When I was waiting for you to ask me out."

I sighed and rubbed my chin in my hand.

"You're right," I said.

"About?"

I chuckled. "It *is* funny. I just had no idea."

She shrugged again. "Well, now you know."

"Now I know."

We ate some more and talked some more about old times, but there was an even bigger gap between us now, because I couldn't stop thinking about this new information. Evelyn had liked me. The whole time. She had liked me. Or at least some of the time, including the time we went to prom. It was as if I had just discovered an old lottery ticket in the bottom of a sock drawer, a scratch-off that was a big winner, but the ticket had an expiration date that had passed years ago.

LILLY MOORE

BACKGROUND

Chapter 25

- - - - - - - - -

One of the first things I learned at college was how difficult it is to get into a fraternity party if you don't have a membership at that fraternity, a membership at another, or boobs. Preferably a pair. With minimal fabric standing between them and the eyes of the guy working the door.

That we lacked any of those prerequisites was why my new friend Brad and I found ourselves trying to slip in through a basement window we had managed to pry open several inches. Fortunately, we were both relatively skinny.

Why was I so desperate to get into the party?

For years, it had been my goal to find a girlfriend. When I went to college, I added to that list of objectives finding a group of close friends—a crew, if you will, who could, among other things, help me navigate the world of dating. Tony, my childhood friend from church, and I had not stayed as close during high school, so I had never had anyone to give me advice when I was trying to date Francesca and Evelyn.

That's why Brad and I found ourselves shoving our bodies through that basement window. We thought we might meet some girls at the party. Maybe I could CFD with one of them. But even if we failed on those counts, nothing bonds two people together like a little breaking and entering. So either way I would end up with a closer friend as a result of the adventure.

We dropped from the window into the corner of a room about five feet from a makeshift bar, several kegs behind it. No one said anything or even looked twice at us. At a party like this one, I realized, there was a high ratio of people who were there to have fun versus people who were there to enforce the rules. And most of the tiny group that fell into the latter category was already stationed at the front door, turning away guys like Brad and me. The partygoers who saw us, the ones who were there purely for fun, couldn't care less about our method of entry.

"You want a beer?" Brad asked.

"Nah," I said.

"I'm gonna get in line."

There were two lines for beer: a guys' line and a girls' line. Fraternity brothers worked the kegs behind the bar and evidently also chose which line to give priority to. The guys' line snaked all the way across the floor of the basement to the stairwell where people entered from the front door upstairs. The girls' line was three girls long.

Anyway, I had decided I didn't want to drink until I was twenty-one. It wasn't like I wanted to take the moral high road. I just didn't like breaking laws. Unless those laws happened to be preventing me from an opportunity to meet girls, in which case I was happy to engage in a bit of trespassing via a basement window.

While Brad waited in line, I made my way to the other side of the basement, where the sticky tile floor dropped several feet to another level that served as a dance floor. It was packed with sweaty revelers. Rap music was blaring. Most people held a red plastic Solo cup in one hand and gripped the body of a dance partner with the other. Unlike high school, I saw, there was not much circle dancing at a frat party. Grinding was rampant. Virtually everyone was paired off. The guys who didn't have a girl to dance with prowled the open floor on the higher level, watching for a girl who didn't have a guy on her already.

I spotted a smile and a wave that seemed to be directed at me. I waved back. It was Paulette, another freshman. I'd hung out with her a few times. Not like "we should hang out sometime" hanging out. Just with a group or whatever. She motioned me over to where she was dancing with her friends.

In contrast to the semi-intoxicated bros prowling the perimeter, I didn't want to accost a girl I had never met with a proposition to dance. So Paulette was an ideal candidate for CFDing. After all, she was probably here in search of a dance partner, right? Maybe even a boyfriend? I mean, why else would you come to a frat party? Plus, I wasn't going to grind on her. I would just put my hands on her hips and then we would sway back and forth together. It would be fun. Good old-fashioned CFDing. Maybe that's why she had motioned me to come over in the first place. She wanted to dance with a boy she knew. A boy like me.

It took me a full twenty minutes to work up the courage. I would tell myself: at the end of this song. No, at the end of *this* song. And so forth.

Finally, I just did it, like tearing off a Band-Aid. All at once I took a step forward on my fake leg so I was only a few inches away from her, placing my hands on her waist and trying to smile a friendly rather than nervous smile. She immediately snapped back, pushing my hands away like she was ripping off a pair of pants she had just discovered to be infested with spiders. "Sorry," she said, slowing down a little as if she was worried she had overreacted. "I just don't want to dance like that."

The way she had instantly shoved away my hands, as if they were too grotesque to allow near her body, as if they were infected with some contagious disease, was more personal and painful than the worst-case scenario I could have imagined.

I was so shocked that for a moment I dropped my mask of confidence; the hurt was written on my face. All that time I had wasted building up my nerve. That entire internal-monologue pep talk had been for nothing.

In fact, worse than for nothing. It had led me to rejection, a violent, physical rejection.

Getting rejected by a girl you are trying to dance with is different from getting rejected by one you asked out on a date. Not necessarily worse or better, just different. When a girl says no to a date, you presume there was some logic behind her decision. She made an evaluation of you in her mind, summing up your traits, her attraction to you, your past history, your five-year plan, the make and model of your car, etc., and then she gave you her answer: no. But when a girl rejects your advance on the dance floor, it is something deeper, more instinctive, more visceral. She is at a fundamental gut level not attracted to you. In fact, she is in some way repelled by you, by your smell, by your presence, by the feeling of your body touching hers. Her rejection of you is precognitive, a pure animal reflex. The dance floor rejection has a stronger physical charge, then: *Your body is not enough. I don't want it near mine.* And this charge is amplified, I think, if you happen to be an amputee, because it throws a spark on the kindling of insecurity you were already harboring concerning the shape of your body.

At any rate, I could not—I would not—dance in the presence of Paulette and her friends after that rejection. I was angry and hurt and humiliated. I waved a wordless good-night and turned to go find Brad.

Paulette grabbed my arm. "Wait. Stay and dance with us some more!" She was smiling. I couldn't tell if she was trying to make up for the way she had made me feel or if she was just completely oblivious to it.

I offered no explanation. That I was walking away communicated everything I had to say.

I found Brad. "I'm leaving."

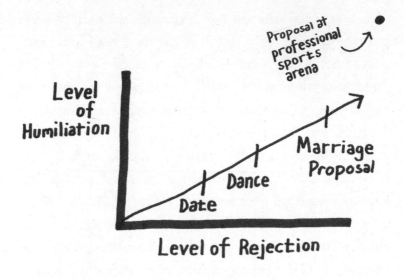

Level of Humiliation

Date — Dance — Marriage Proposal — Proposal at professional sports arena

Level of Rejection

"Now?"

I nodded tersely.

"You want me to come with you?"

"If you want."

He looked around, surveying the room, and then back at me. "All right. Hold on." He downed his beer in a single gulp, tossing the cup into a nearby trash can, and we left out the front door. Despite my anger, or perhaps because of it, I couldn't help but look over my shoulder and smile at the bouncers as we exited, pushing through the crowd that was trying to get in. Suckers.

Brad and I sat outside and I told him what had happened and he listened. I had to admit: Having a friend to talk about it with did *not* make me feel better. Not completely, that is. But it did feel better than holding it all inside.

Chapter 26

- - - - - - - -

As you may be aware, most formal dating relationships in college, in the rare cases that they actually exist, start with hooking up. If a couple hooks up enough times, and they find themselves waking up beside each other with frequency, and—here's the major turning point—*going to the dining hall for breakfast together,* they may be headed toward an actual boyfriend-girlfriend-type relationship. But as I said, it's rare for couples to pair off in this formal way on a college campus, so what you get instead are what I call Ambiguous College Relationships. In an ACR, sometimes you get drunk and make out, then don't talk for a couple of days, then have coffee together, then don't talk for a while, then get drunk and make out again, then wonder if you may in fact be dating this person now, or whether it is merely a "friends with benefits" situation. I lump all these relationships under the umbrella of emotional confusion that is the ACR.

Anyway, since I didn't drink or, for that matter, hook

up, I still had not even kissed a girl. I was a little old-fashioned in that I was actually trying to go on, you know, dates. The difficult thing about asking a girl on a date at college is that it's rare to be in a one-on-one conversation with her. You're always in a group. A table at the cafeteria. A circle standing around after class. A mass of nude streakers. My point is, it's tough to ask a girl out, or even to say *We should hang out sometime*, because there are other ears listening. Not only might she reject you, she might reject you *in front of an audience*.

It took several months past forever to spot such a perfect moment with Lilly, this girl I'd met at a Christian event on campus. She was cute, and she never asked me how I lost my leg, which I took as a sign my disability wasn't important to her. Finally, one night, we were both in the Pizza Hut in the University Center, and I saw her get up from her table to go to the bathroom. I got up from my own table and followed her. No, perverts, I wasn't following her to the bathroom. I was just trying to make sure the vector of her movement and the vector of mine had an intersection at the end of the aisle. Fortunately, I'm pretty good with vectors.

"Oh hey, what's up, Lilly!" I said, as if to say, *I'm so pleasantly surprised to see you here at Pizza Hut and furthermore that our vectors happened to intersect at the end of this aisle!*

She smiled. "Josh! Hi!"

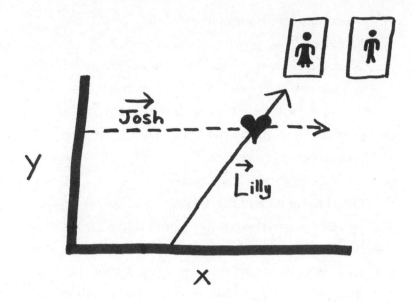

"What are you up to?"

"Just eating some za."

"Excuse me?"

"Za. It's an abbreviation for pizza."

"Oh...okay."

She chuckled at her abbreviation.

"My biffil—I mean, my BFFL, best friend for life— Sadie Bickley, see her over there waving—hi, biffil!—we like to make abbreves, I mean, abbreviations—for everything. Saves a lot of time."

"Life is short, I guess."

"So true."

"Might as well use every syllable to the fullest."

She nodded. "Again, so true. What are you up to tonight?"

"Meeting up with some friends later. You?"

"Samesies."

"Now see, there it seemed like you *added* a syllable."

"But 'samesies' is so much more fun to say."

"Think how much time you've wasted saying that extra syllable twice in the last ten seconds."

"Jeez, I guess you're right," she said. "Those are seconds I am never going to get back."

"Good thing we had this talk."

She nodded, mock-serious. "Good thing."

"Anyway, great to see you," I said, swinging my hand out sideways to wind up for a slap–speed handshake.

"You, too." She smiled as our hands collided and pulled back, the fingertips locking like yin and yang. She took a step away but I didn't let go of her hand, as if I had just remembered something I wanted to tell her.

"Hey. We should hang out sometime."

"Totes."

I'm not going to lie. It all felt pretty smooth.

But I took the smoothness down a few notches by adding, "What's your last name? I'll look you up in the student directory and drop you an e-mail."

Brad set his fork down on his cafeteria tray. He was skeptical. "Lilly? The girl who was at Pizza Hut?"

"Yeah, dude, she has this, I don't know, this *X factor*. Like this spark or vivaciousness."

230

"Vivaciousness, huh?"

"Yeah." I smiled. "And she would hate that word. She likes abbrev—never mind. You just have to meet her."

"I'm not sure you guys would look right together."

"How so?"

"Think about it. She dresses like a model for J.Crew, like she owns a boat. You dress like *you are* the crew. Like you work on a boat."

"Very funny. I prefer to say that I dress like a model for Goodwill, thank you very much."

"Well, let me know how it goes."

"I will. How are things with Avery?"

Avery was the girl with whom Brad was in an ACR. They had dated some early in high school and by coincidence both ended up at William and Mary. Sometimes they made out late at night. Other times they stayed up late having Deep Discussions, as college freshmen like to do.

"Complicated."

"They always are."

I was waiting for Lilly at the coffee shop, wearing khaki shorts that I had made by cutting off a pair of normal khaki pants, paired with a vintage T-shirt from a city council campaign that took place in the early nineties. I had been using my artificial leg less and less; the campus was just too big to walk on it. Crutches were easier. So that's how I was rolling today: crutches and one leg. Lilly arrived also wearing khakis, in her case a fitted khaki skirt and a light blue button-up cardigan. It was probably cashmere, and I wished I could touch it. You know, to find out for sure.

"Hey," she said.

"Hi," I said.

We hugged.

She ordered coffee and I got an Italian soda flavored with raspberry syrup. As we sat down, I couldn't help but notice the way her curves pushed against her well-tailored J.Crew ensemble. In church when I was growing up, we were always taught that you couldn't help noticing a girl's body. If your gaze *lingers*, however, that's when the noticing has turned into the sin of lust. So whenever you notice a girl's body, you are supposed to "bounce" your eyes and look at something else. But the only thing I noticed was that my eyes kept bouncing back.

We started talking, diving into a three-hour conversation of topics both deep and meaningful, the sort of discussion you hear a lot of on a college campus. Our coffee dates became a weekly event for the next month and a half. My instincts said things were going well. Which I should have taken as a sign that they weren't.

Chapter 27

— — — — — — — —

It was always tough to tear my friend Kyle away from his studying to do things other people would consider important, like, for example, eating. But tonight, we'd successfully extracted him from his books, and he, Brad, and I were sitting in the cafeteria ingesting calories and swapping stories about high school relationships. I told them a little about Francesca and Evelyn.

"So what did they say?" Kyle asked.

"When?" I replied.

"When you told them you liked them?"

I laughed. "Yeah, right! I could never tell them I liked them! You know how much risk of rejection that is?"

"Dude," said Kyle, brushing blond curls off his forehead. "You're telling me you've never had a DTR?"

"A D-T-what?"

"A 'define the relationship' talk. Where you tell a girl you like her. You talk about whether you two want to be together. That kind of stuff."

"Um, nope."

"Did you kiss either of them?"

"No, of course not. I've never kissed anyone."

"Yeah, that's probably why you've never had a girl-friend. Brad, back me up here."

"I'm with Kyle," said Brad, leaning forward. "If you never tell a girl you like her or make out with her, I mean, how's she going to know?"

I stroked my chin. "But what if she doesn't like me?"

"It happens," said Kyle. "That's life. But if you don't have a DTR, you're never going to know if she likes you, too."

"I guess so."

"I know so," said Kyle.

"How long have you been having those coffee dates with Lilly?" asked Brad.

"I don't know. Maybe six weeks," I said.

"And no DTR?" asked Kyle.

"No. Of course not," I said.

Kyle and Brad exchanged a glance.

"Dude, it's time," said Kyle.

"For a DTR? No way! I need to give it a few more months!"

"That's what you've been telling yourself your whole life." His tone was friendly, but the truth struck deep.

"Yeah," I said thoughtfully. "I guess you're right. But even if I say yes to it now...when I'm with her I'll choke."

"Don't worry about that," said Kyle.

"Too late, already worried."

"That's because you haven't heard about my boots yet."

"Um, what?"

"I've got a pair of steel-toed boots under my bunk bed in my dorm," explained Kyle. "The next time you see Lilly, if you don't have a DTR, I am going to put on those boots and I am going to kick you as hard as I possibly can in your balls."

"Excuse me?"

"You heard me."

"You're serious?"

"In your balls."

"Steel?"

"Yes, it's an iron alloy. I'm sure you've heard of it."

"Are you joking?"

"Do I look like I'm joking?"

"He doesn't look like he's joking," interjected Brad.

"Did I mention I was the starting forward of my high school soccer team?" asked Kyle. "I've got a mean left foot."

"The next time I see her?"

"Or else."

"Dude..." I said, incredulous.

"Steel. Your balls. Think about it."

I sighed, surrendering. "Okay, you leave me no other choice. Next time I see her it is."

"You do that, my boots stay under my bed."

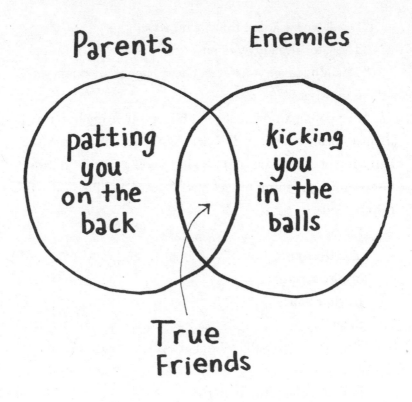

Parents

Enemies

patting you on the back

kicking you in the balls

True Friends

"Thanks, I guess?"

"What else are friends for?"

I began by writing and memorizing a speech to give to Lilly, which I rehearsed endlessly to make it sound as spontaneous and organic as possible. The content of the speech? If you read the entry for the word "beautiful" in the thesaurus, you'll have the basic idea.

I figured we needed a venue change for this date. A coffee shop wasn't grand enough for the sweeping romanticism of my intentions and feelings. So I e-mailed Lilly and suggested that we go to the college's boathouse, where we could borrow a canoe and paddle around Lake Matoaka, the serene (and romantic!) body of water tucked in the woods at the back of campus.

She agreed. I told Brad and Kyle: *This is it. I am going for it. We are going to row out to the middle of the lake and confess our love for each other.*

On the day of the big date, I knocked on her door and found a little powwow of Lilly and her friends on the rug in the center of her dorm room. I was too nervous about my upcoming speech, however, to pay any mind to the weirdness of the situation on the floor.

"Ready?" I asked.

"Yeppers," she said. Indeed she was, decked out in a pair of Sperry Top-Siders and a coat with anchor-embossed gold buttons.

Her friend Sarah Martin, who was wearing too much makeup as usual, asked me, "What are you all doing?"

Not until later, when I would play back her question in my mind, would I hear how scripted it sounded, how well rehearsed. Not at all spontaneous or organic.

"Canoeing," I said.

"Oh, can I come?" she asked.

Right on cue, Lilly and all her friends looked up at me as if their very lives were hanging on my reply.

"Um, sure," I said, trying to hide my disappointment.

Again, I hadn't noticed this was clearly a setup. I was

too busy thinking about a steel-toed boot that would be dropping my voice two octaves if I didn't find a way to have a DTR today, and how this addition of a third wheel on the date would make the conversation considerably more challenging. I mean, can you imagine a more uncomfortable social situation than having an uninvolved third party sitting in the middle of a canoe while the two other passengers hash out the details of what may turn out to be a completely one-sided romantic relationship?

But then, a miracle occurred. Lilly's BFFL, Sadie, needed a ride to the bank. Lilly was the only one with a car. Lilly had to give Sadie a ride, drop Sadie off, *and then drive back* before we could go canoeing. I pounced.

"Can I come...keep you company?"

Lilly looked around at her group of friends. This was apparently a contingency they had not planned for. They had protected Lilly from being alone with me on top of a body of water in a romantic piece of floating fiberglass, yes, but not from this simple errand.

"Oh, um—the thing is..." Lilly struggled to find an excuse. But none came. "Sure, of course."

After we dropped Sadie at the bank, I moved into the front seat of Lilly's Volkswagen convertible. The roof was down. I had a window of approximately two minutes before we'd be back at her dorm to get Sarah and go to the lake. So I got right down to business.

"Lilly, there's something I have to tell you," I said, raising my voice over the wind.

She winced. Like she had been afraid this might happen. Undeterred, I spoke quickly, accelerating my words to be sure I finished my speech before we reached her dorm. As I spoke, I noticed that she was also accelerating—accelerating her car.

"Lilly, I think you're incredibly beautiful, funny, smart, interesting, clever, pretty, stylish—"

"Josh, no," she whimpered.

"Let me finish." I had worked long and hard on these lines and I wasn't about to end my performance prematurely. "Where was I?"

"Um, stylish?"

"Yeah—stylish, cool, fun, kind, charming, gorgeous…"

Based on her response so far, I knew this conversation was nose-diving, in complete free fall. MAYDAY MAYDAY. But Kyle and Brad had raised a good point: With Francesca and Evelyn, I could only look back and wonder, what if? I would only ever have a chance with Lilly if I took the plunge and told her I liked her.

"…cute, punctual, creative, intelligent, fashionable…"

And in my mind, that meant dropping this adjective bomb. I guess I believed that the more my speech sounded like an actual thesaurus entry, the more romantic it was. As if the number of adjectives a person uses to describe his affection is directly proportional to the chances it will be reciprocated.

"And that's why I can't stop thinking about you, all day, every single day." Since she didn't seem eager to turn

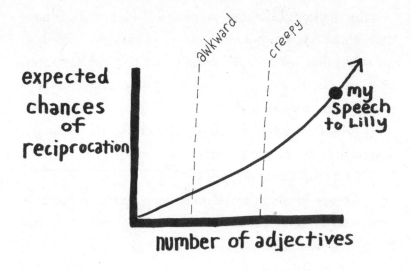

expected chances of reciprocation

number of adjectives

awkward

creepy

my speech to Lilly

her head and kiss me or anything, the speech ended in a whimper. "And I . . . just wanted you to know that."

"Oh, Josh," she said. Her tone sounded like I had just told her I was facing a life-threatening illness.

I was silent.

"The fact is," she said, "I have a crush on Sam Dayne."

Sam Dayne? Sam . . . *Dayne*? That stung. I knew she had liked him during the fall semester, and they had dated a little, but I had heard through the rumor mill that he wasn't much interested in her—he being both hilarious *and* a member of the football team, and therefore having his pick of the girls on campus—and she had since moved on. That last part, at least, turned out to not be true.

"Bummer," I said.

By this time we were parking in front of her dorm. Sarah was standing outside, waiting for our boat outing.

"You still want to go canoeing?" Lilly asked.

I'm sure she expected me to say no. I mean, who in his right mind would want to keep hanging out after that? But partly out of a misguided need to demonstrate that her rejection had little effect on me, and partly because I knew how uncomfortable it would be for her to sit in a canoe with me now and I wanted her to suffer through every bit of awkwardness possible as punishment for not liking me back, I said yes, I would very much still like to go canoeing.

As it turned out, the only person I was punishing was myself. The canoes were two-person, so I ended up with a kayak while Lilly and Sarah shared the canoe. They were terrible paddlers, mostly spinning in circles and repeatedly colliding with the shoreline. So I just drifted behind in my kayak, always staying within earshot so as to delay the flood of gossip Lilly was no doubt eager to unleash. As long as they knew I was listening, my humiliation would remain a secret. You can't talk about someone behind his back when he's literally, you know, right behind your back—or your boat, as the case may be.

I plopped my tray of food down and laid my crutches on the floor underneath the table. Kyle and Brad were already seated, eating. Kyle had a pile of textbooks in front of him. They looked up at me, eyebrows raised.

I gave them one word. "Disastrous."

They gave each other a look.

"What?" I asked.

They looked at the floor.

"What?" I demanded.

"That's kind of what we expected," confessed Kyle.

"You expected this?"

"Well, we knew she didn't like you," he said.

I held up my hand in a stop sign. "Hold up. You *knew*?"

"That's an exaggeration," said Brad. "I mean, well, we thought, based on how you described your conversations, that she had put you in the Friend Zone."

I threw my hands in the air. These were supposed to be my friends! My two best friends! And they had betrayed me, sent me right into the lion's den to get devoured.

"Are you kidding me?"

"Whoa, hear me out," said Brad.

I folded my arms. "Fine. I'm listening."

"We didn't know for sure. I mean, *maybe* she did like you. We didn't know. We just guessed that—"

"That she didn't like me and you would screw me over?" I interrupted.

"Look, Josh," said Kyle. "You're what? Eighteen years old? And you've never told a girl you liked her. You've never had a DTR."

That much was true. I stayed silent.

"You needed to try it. You needed to tell a girl how you felt about her. And if she doesn't like you, so what?"

"So what?" I said. "So what? It's horrible. I feel like she tore out my heart and threw it on the ground."

Kyle held up a finger. "You *feel* like that, yes. And we've all been there and we all know how much it sucks. But here's the thing: She didn't literally tear out your heart. It's actually still beating inside your chest."

"Thanks for the helpful diagnosis, Dr. Premed," I intoned sarcastically.

"No, what I mean is, you're still alive. You got rejected. And you survived. Sure, it hurts. And it's not something you'd want to do every day. But now you know you can live through it. And the next time a girl comes along, maybe it won't be quite as terrifying to tell her you like her."

I pursed my lips. I hated to admit it, but they were right. I had been rejected. And it sucked. But I had survived. And none of it would've happened in the first place if it weren't for these friends. I was grateful. I would never admit it out loud, of course. But I did appreciate what they had done, how they had helped me. They had pushed me out of the nest. I didn't fly, exactly. I basically fell straight down and smacked into the ground. But at least I was out of that nest.

Unfortunately, I was not quite finished humiliating myself with Lilly.

Chapter 28

– – – – – – – – –

As I've explained, when it comes to girls, often the best strategy is to take whatever I think I should do and then do the opposite. Following my own instincts, I've found, generally leads to disaster.

And Lilly was no exception.

I didn't get a cell phone until after freshman year of college. I was, like, one of the last people in my generation to get one. So I was a little behind the learning curve. I did not know, for example, that caller ID was a standard feature on all cell phones. And this created problems.

I had Lilly's number from when we used to go on coffee dates. And even though she'd explicitly told me she did not like me, that she liked Sam Dayne, and even though we'd had the most awkward boating date ever, a date so uncomfortable that any guy of at least average intelligence would shrink away from contact with that girl ever again, even in spite of all this, I figured we should keep in touch over the summer. Just in case, you know, she changed her mind. So I called her. Every. Single. Day. She never picked up, though, so I figured she was just busy. I did not realize that her cell phone was recording each missed call, and furthermore, that she was most likely ignoring all the calls in the first place. I didn't want her to know how often I was calling, though—I might have been naive, but I wasn't stupid—so I left a voice mail only once a month, imagining she'd think I was *calling* only once a month, too. "Hey there, it's Josh, just wanted to say hi. . . . Haven't heard back from you since I called last month." I'm usually pretty good with technology, but somehow it took me the entire summer to figure out that my cell phone had caller ID, that I could ignore incoming calls from people with whom I did not want to speak, and, most importantly, that my phone recorded all missed and ignored calls in a list that I could review at any time. I distinctly remember the moment when I realized this. I had just parked my car and was still sitting in the driver's seat. I thought: I have been calling her daily. All summer. That's what, a hundred calls? I almost threw up on the dashboard.

After that, I tried to stop bothering Lilly. I still liked her, of course; that didn't go away. But I figured I'd already put her through more than the FDA-recommended lifetime dose of uncomfortable situations. So I kept my crush under wraps from her. We hung out in the same circles for the rest of college, but I made sure only my closest friends knew I still liked her. That is, until one of them told her.

But I'm getting ahead of our story. Back to this cell phone caller ID disaster. Yeah, my instincts aren't the best. But they aren't the worst, either. And I know that thanks to Stella. Stella the Stalker.

Anyway, Stella and I had Statistics together sophomore year. The class was at nine thirty in the morning, which, for college, is really, really early. But I was also really, really interested in statistics, so I signed up. Every morning before class, I would eat breakfast by myself in the cafeteria. A few weeks into the semester, I noticed that when I got up to leave, this girl Stella—I didn't actually know her name yet, so at the time she was just the emaciated-looking girl with stringy brown hair and a penchant for what appeared to be homemade dresses—would stand up, too, from her table across the room. She would follow me outside and then walk about three feet behind me all the way to class. I am not exaggerating here, people. Three feet. Silently. Never said a word. Just followed right behind me for the ten-minute walk from the cafeteria to the math building. After a few weeks of this, I couldn't stand it any longer—I turned around and introduced myself. She took this as an invitation to walk side by side with me, which she started doing each day, still in complete silence. Sometimes, I would glance over at her desk during Statistics, and 100 percent of the time (I was able to make this calculation thanks to what I learned in the class, obviously) she was staring at me with creepy, saucer-sized eyes.

This all got to be pretty annoying, so I started trying to fake her out at breakfast. I'd get up and put my tray in the dirty-dish rack but then duck back into the food line to get a banana. Sometimes I thought I had fooled her and would be able to walk alone, but inevitably I found her waiting on the sidewalk somewhere along my route to class. She would be standing there by herself, and when I walked by, she would wordlessly fall into step beside me, like this was all totally normal.

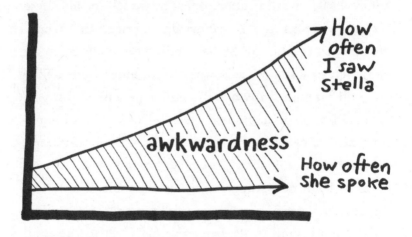

It got worse. I played intramural soccer every Sunday afternoon on a team with my friends. I played on my crutches. I wasn't really good or anything, but I did all right. Anyway, when I got home from my games each week, I would always have an e-mail waiting from her. The body of the e-mail would be blank; the subject line would be the score of the game with my team listed first, like

"1–2" or "4–0." But I *never actually saw her on the sidelines*, so I couldn't figure out where she was getting this information. Later in the season, I realized she must live in the dorm that overlooked the field. In other words, she was sitting at her window, watching all my games and keeping track of the score. During time-outs, I would take quick glances to look for her face looming in one of the windows. I never did see it, though.

And it got worse still. She learned my class schedule and combined it with her walking routes so that in between my classes we would pass each other on the sidewalks. She figured out my weekend interests and I began spotting her sitting alone in the theater when I went with my friends to watch a movie or comedian on campus. This was when I started worrying she might be watching me sleep or something, and when I decided it all had to stop.

I had become so aware of her movements that I was basically reverse-stalking her. Like, I knew that every Wednesday at one o'clock she would be in the lobby of the campus center, sitting on the couch pretending to read while she actually watched the front doors, waiting for me to walk by. So that Wednesday, I walked right up to her in the lobby of the campus center.

"We need to talk," I said.

From my tone, I thought it was pretty clear that the exchange wasn't going to turn out real well for her, but she just smiled shyly, like this was the moment she'd been dreaming of for many months. She closed her book and slid it into the canvas bag sitting on the floor beside her Velcro-fastened sneakers.

"I would be pleased to talk with you, Joshua," she said. She looked around like she was wondering if our conversation might be too special to hold in a crowded place like this one.

"Okay, here's the thing," I said, looking down at her on the couch. "You know how every morning you leave breakfast at the same time as me?"

Her face fell. "You noticed that?"

"*Noticed?* Of course—how could I not—of course I noticed! You walk beside me *every single day.*"

"I meant how we finish eating at the same time," she said. "I was hoping you would just think it was coincidence."

"Um, no, didn't think it was coincidence," I said. "I also noticed how you know my class schedule and follow me around between classes."

She didn't attempt to deny it. Instead, she tried to distract me with flattery.

"I find pleasure in being with you. You are different from other men."

It was strange. I'd spent my whole life trying to become a man, but when she actually used that word, it made me shiver with discomfort.

"That kind of thing is not normal," I said.

"But if I didn't follow you around, how would I get to see you?" she asked. She looked genuinely confused, like everything so far had been part of the early stages of a normal relationship, and the only problem here was my not being comfortable with her entirely reasonable actions.

I decided two things in that moment. Number one, she needed a wake-up call. Number two, I would be her alarm clock.

"Okay, check it out. There are three types of social encounters," I began. "Number one, a planned encounter. That's like when you meet someone for lunch or coffee at a set time and place. Number two, a random encounter. That's like when you just happen to walk by someone on the way to class. With me so far?"

She nodded.

"The third type is a planned encounter disguised to look like a random encounter. That's like when you stand in the grass and wait so you can wave at me when I walk by on my way to English Lit."

She was quiet for a while as she considered this.

"So you don't want to hang out with me anymore," she concluded.

Um, what? When had we ever *hung out*?

It was true, though; I had no interest in hanging out. But I couldn't say so directly. After all, I had experienced my fair share of rejection. I knew how it felt to be in her shoes. In fact, I had made some uncomfortably stalkerish moves myself, what with calling Lilly every day the previous summer. I wanted to believe that calling someone once every twenty-four hours wasn't quite as bad as physically inserting yourself between a guy and his class multiple times each day. But still, I had to have some sympathy for Stella.

"No," I said. "I'm happy to talk to you. I just think we should have more of the type-two encounters and less type-three."

She stood and threw her bag over her shoulder.

"Don't worry," she said. "I will no longer be bothering you."

She said this in a cool tone, as if I should feel bad and argue with her that oh, no, she isn't a bother at all—but the truth was, my daily life would be more pleasant without her.

"Great!" I said. "Or, that is, I mean, it's great that we're on the same page now."

The next morning, I enjoyed an incredibly peaceful walk to Statistics, and then another Stella-less journey back to my dorm. If I had known it would be this easy, I would have explained the three types of social encounters a long time ago. But later that day, as I walked by the library on the way to my next class, I shivered as I passed the spot where she always used to stand. She wasn't there, but I felt sure she was watching me. Maybe I was being paranoid, I told myself. Just to be sure, I looked up at the library and scanned all four floors of windows for her face.

Nothing. Whew! I *was* getting paranoid. I smiled and shook my head as I continued walking. I passed by a tree that had been blocking my view of a few of the windows. That's when I glanced back at the library and saw her face pressed against the glass on the second story. I was so startled that I literally jumped, nearly knocking over some girls walking behind me. I apologized and then looked up at the window again, but she was gone.

When I got back to my dorm, I wrote her an e-mail. "Watching from windows still counts as a type-three encounter."

She replied a few hours later with a four-thousand-word e-mail that contained a summary of every conversation we had ever had, including what each of us had been wearing on that day, as well as her interpretations of the significance of the T-shirts I had chosen (e.g., I wore this shirt on that day because it was the same shirt I was wearing when we met). Her e-mail was creepily written in the third person, referring to herself as "the girl" and me as "the boy." It concluded (eventually) with a promise to neither talk to me nor watch me from any windows ever again.

And Stella was true to her word. After that I saw her only once every couple months, usually at the library if I was there studying or whatever. I'd say *Hi, Stella*, but she would ignore me. Which was kind of awkward—but honestly, less uncomfortable than when she used to follow me around.

The thing I preferred not to admit was how much Stella reminded me of myself: the social awkwardness, the chance meetings that were not actually happening by chance. I mean, I had gone out of my way freshman year of high school to meet Liza Taylor Smith, right?

The truth is, I only thought of Stella as a stalker because I wasn't interested in dating her. If I had been attracted to her, I might have thought her tendency to plan her life around mine was cute. That's the thing about us human beings: If we have a crush on someone, that person's every behavior attracts us even more. But if we don't like that person, the very same behavior will annoy us.

Chapter 29

A lot of people want their first kiss to be special. I just wanted mine to be during this lifetime. I had missed my chances for special already. I missed them at the waterfall with Francesca and at prom with Evelyn. I was twenty years old, for crying out loud, and I'd still never kissed anyone. I didn't care about special anymore. I needed only a pair of willing female lips and a little bit of courage.

I found both late one night when I was walking this girl Katie back from a party. Katie was a friend. But attractive enough. I was still head over heel[9] for Lilly, of course, but I needed to get this first-kiss thing out of the way. What if Lilly changed her mind about me and we started dating? Obviously, I would need to have some skills to impress her. I wouldn't want my tongue flopping around all awkwardly in Lilly's mouth, revealing my status as a total kissing n00b.

---

[9] Heel, singular. Not a typo.

I was sitting with Katie on a couch in her dorm.

"So I would kind of like to kiss you right now," I said.

"Really?" She looked rather startled. But not uninterested.

"Yeah," I confirmed.

"Maybe you should give it a try."

"The thing is..." I glanced at the wall. "I kind of like this other girl."

She drew back, her tone going cold. "So why would you want to kiss me?"

"Well, I mean, I like you, too. Not quite the way I like her, but, that is, I'm definitely attracted to you. Yeah, you're really pretty."

She inclined her head.

"Go on."

"I've always had a little thing for you, and you know, it just feels right."

She raised her eyebrows.

"So?" I asked.

"So what?"

"Do you think we should kiss?"

"Let's give it a shot and find out."

I frowned. "Yeah. About that. So...I've never kissed anyone before."

"Never?"

"No."

"Wow."

"What?"

"It's just that—how old are you?"

"Twenty."

"Hmmm."

"So...does that mean yes?"

And on it went like this for, I am not kidding you, over thirty minutes. Back and forth discussion about whether we should kiss, what implications it might have for our friendship, what our respective friend groups would think about it, whether as a Christian I was allowed to kiss her as an atheist, etc. It was all very scientific and analytical. Just the way I like it. But kisses are not supposed to be scientific. Or analytical. In fact, the longer you examine a kiss under a microscope, the smaller becomes its magic.

"So when are you gonna make a move on me?" she asked.

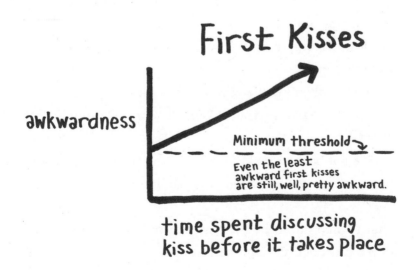

First Kisses

awkwardness

Minimum threshold

Even the least awkward first kisses are still, well, pretty awkward.

time spent discussing kiss before it takes place

"Like I've been telling you, I really don't know how," I said. "You have to get us started."

We sat in silence for a few moments, and then suddenly there was something wet and slimy inserting itself between my lips, prying open my jaw and exploring the concavities of my mouth. I realized that this was...her tongue. We were kissing.

Having never kissed before, I wasn't aware that you are supposed to close your eyes. Big mistake. Her face was one inch from mine, and at that distance, I could see every pore, every eyebrow follicle, ever wrinkle of melanin-hued epidermis. I shut my eyes in horror.

"I'm not sure if this is allowed," she said, grabbing my hand and placing it firmly over her breast. For a moment, I was too shocked to respond. Not shocked at her actions, shocked at how it felt. I had always assumed breasts would feel squishy and heavy, like a cross between a stress ball and a water-bed mattress. What I felt instead was unexpectedly soft.

That's when I realized what I was touching.

"No!" I snapped my hand back. "Definitely not allowed."

We got back to making out, and by the time I made it home the sky was beginning to turn light.

That turned out to be my first and only kiss in college. I didn't do much dating there, either, because, as I said,

I still liked Lilly. But I tried to keep it a secret. She was in my circle of friends, and I didn't want to make things weird for her. Only Brad and Kyle and my other close friends knew I still liked her. And they didn't say anything. That is, until senior year. See, senior year we were all twenty-one. And alcohol, among many other side effects, reduces people's ability to keep secrets.

One Friday night, my guy friends and I were coming out of a bar. I should specify that this was not a cool bar by any means, but rather the karaoke night at a bar on the first floor of a hotel near campus. But in a small town like Williamsburg, there isn't always a lot to do, so watching old people sing karaoke at a hotel on Friday night is, believe it or not, sometimes your best option.

I should also remind you that I didn't drink at all until I was twenty-one, and even after I was twenty-one, I still had a religious hangover that made me afraid of more than one or two beers. So although some of my friends were a bit tipsy, I was pretty sober at this point. We stumbled out into the night air, and guess who was in the parking lot? That's right, Lilly and some of her girlfriends. Hellos and "What are you guys up to tonights" were exchanged.

Side note: You've heard of a stage whisper, right? The term comes from live theater, like a play or whatever, when one actor pulls another aside and whispers to him loudly enough that the audience can hear it. The audience is meant to believe that even though the whisper had enough volume to fill up the auditorium, the other characters onstage could not hear it; it was a private conversation between the two characters who are "whispering" to each other.

Drunk people are prone to accidental stage whispers, inadvertently underestimating the volume of their whispering. Upon seeing Lilly in the parking lot, my friend Ben, who had apparently thrown back quite a few drinks while watching the karaoke, stage-whispered to me in a voice that was clearly audible to everyone in the parking lot—and probably everyone back inside the bar, too—*"Dude, it's your girl!"*

Just in case it was not 100 percent clear whom he was talking about, he pointed his finger at Lilly, too, while tapping his other hand on my shoulder. I turned to Ben and whispered in his ear (an actual whisper, not a stage one), *"Shut up, dude, she can hear you."* Drunk though he was, he could hear the urgency in my voice, and he shut up. I relaxed a little. It was over.

Or so I thought.

A week later I was hanging out at Lilly and Sadie's apartment. It was late at night, and there were just four of us there: Lilly, Sadie, Brad (my roommate of three years), and I. We were sitting on the couches in their living room. And then, out of nowhere, Lilly dropped the bomb.

"What was your friend Ben saying the other night?" she asked me.

I was pretty sure I knew what she was talking about. But I hoped, I really hoped, that I did not. So I played dumb.

"What night?" I asked, putting a puzzled expression on my face.

"You know, the other night," she said.

"Uh...no..."

Sadie and Brad were silent as they watched this exchange play out.

"You know, in the parking lot," said Lilly. "As you guys were leaving karaoke?"

She had me cornered.

So I tried to acknowledge the night without having to answer her question. "Oh, right, that was a fun night. What did you all end up doing?"

But Lilly was undeterred by my attempt to change the subject. She pressed forward. "So, what did he say to you?"

I was trapped. She was obviously not going to let me off without answering her question. But I couldn't tell her the truth. I couldn't tell her that he'd said *Dude, it's your girl*, because doing so would force me to reveal that I'd still had a crush on her all these years.

But I couldn't lie. Could I? I am not a big fan of lying. For one thing, I'm not really good at it. I don't exactly know how to lie, and I am always afraid that I'll forget which lie I told to which person and get caught later when my stories didn't match up.

But this, this was an impossible dilemma.

So I did the unthinkable: I lied.

"Oh—oh yeah," I stammered. "He—he was saying— he was saying how he had forgotten his driver's license and he had to go back to the dorm and get it so they would let him into the bar."

See? Told you I was a bad liar.

It was, like, the worst lie ever. Ben had clearly said *Dude, it's your girl*, and everyone knew it. I could've at least come up with a lie that sounded like a similar phrase. For example, I could have told her that he had said *Hats off to the Duke of Earl*. Nonsensical but similar. Instead, I made up this lie, which was an absolutely implausible story because, oh yeah, *we had just walked out of the bar*. Obviously, he had used his license to get inside in the first place.

But mercifully, Lilly did not realize I was lying. Or, more likely, she chose not to call me out on it. She glanced over at Sadie, a glance I couldn't read but wished I could because I imagine it contained oh-so-much meaning, and then she said, "Oh, okay. His ID. I see."

I changed the subject, and a few minutes later Brad and I said our good-nights. During the walk back to our dorm, we analyzed the earth-shattering conversation that had just gone down. My adrenaline was still pumping. We wondered: Did she actually know what Ben had said? Did she know I was lying? Did she know I'd had a crush on her for the entire four years of college?

HYPOTHESIS

Although subject never had romantic feelings toward me, it appears she overheard the conversation between Ben and me after our egress from the karaoke bar, and therefore that subject was forcing me either to admit liking her or to lie when she inquired as to what Ben had said.

Further investigation is required to discover her motives.

INVESTIGATION

Chapter 30

— — — — — — — — — —

I knew that Lilly liked Sam, the football player, not me. I got that. But what I didn't know was why she called me out that night in her apartment, forcing me to lie about my conversation with Ben. I was also curious whether she knew that I was lying, and whether she knew I liked her during all of college, not just freshman year when we were going on coffee dates.

Up until this time, all the girls I had investigated in this study had been from my hometown, so I was able to connect with them face-to-face while I was home for the holidays. But I knew Lilly from college, and she lived a few states away now. So I tracked her down on Facebook and wrote her this message:

To: Lilly
From: Josh
Lilly,
What's up? Hope you are well.

So I am doing this life project thingy to seek closure and forgiveness. (Whoooa — is it me or did this message just get weird?!)

OK. So.

One night senior year at W&M we were all standing outside the Hospitality House. My friend Ben, who was sort of drunk, pointed at you and whispered (very loudly) to me, "Dude, it's your girl." And I was like, "Shut up, she can hear you."

A few weeks later I was hanging out at your apartment at King and Queen and you called me out on it.

"What did your friend say to you in front of Hospitality House?" you asked.

This put me in an awkward position. I had basically had a crush on you for all four years of college, but after freshman year I tried to keep this a secret from you and your friends since we ran in the same circles and I didn't want to make things uncomfortable for you. Perhaps you suspected this all along. Or perhaps this is the first you've heard of it.

Anyway, obviously Ben had been referring to my crush on you, but I couldn't tell you that, so I lied and told you something about him forgetting his ID. I'm not a fan of lying, so first, I wanted to ask your forgiveness.

Second, I wanted to ask if you remember the incident, and if so: Did you actually hear what

Ben said at Hospitality House? Did you know I was lying?

All these years, I've wondered if you did.

Anyway, I know this is a very, very strange message, so feel free to just delete it. But if you would like to reply with any insight (large or small) into what you remember of that conversation, I would be most grateful for the emotional closure.
Cheers,
Josh

I held my breath for a couple of days while I waited to see if she would respond.[10] And then, one night I logged on to Facebook and there it was:

To: Josh
From: Lilly
josh it's so good to hear from you! now, as for this lie you say you told me, i can't say i remember the incident but i am flattered. ah, college. and of course i forgive you — no worries at all!
glad you are doing well,
Lilly

To paraphrase Elie Wiesel, in relationships, the opposite of love is not hate. The opposite of love is indifference.

---

[10] Figuratively speaking. Otherwise I'd be dead. Just saying.

Having no feelings at all. Not caring either way. Hate, at least, requires a foundation of emotional involvement with the relationship.

Which is not to say that Lilly hated me, or that she had complete apathy toward me, but I had to admit: It sort of stung to learn that not only was that conversation about Ben not a big deal to her, *she didn't even remember it*. That was how little it mattered to her. It was, for me, this big, watershed moment in my life, a defining conversation in Lilly's and my (admittedly one-sided) relationship. But for her, it did not even make enough of an impression that the memory was worth saving.

But I knew I shouldn't be surprised. She liked the other guy. Not me. And though her reply on Facebook wasn't the insightful answer I was hoping for, she did give me an answer. That's the thing about life: Just because we don't get the answers we're hoping for doesn't mean they aren't answers nonetheless.

SASHA
WRIGHT

BACKGROUND

Chapter 31

"Can I ask you a question?"

"Sure," said the tall blond girl.

"Why are you wearing a crown right now?" I asked.

"Oh, that?" Her eyes darted upward, as if she could see through her forehead to the tiara that was perched there. "I have to wear it whenever I'm on official business."

As a general rule, I did not walk up to pretty girls and start talking to them like this. The summer after college, I had done some soul-searching and decided I was fed up with dating. Too much rejection. Too much trouble. Not that I didn't want a girlfriend anymore. Just that it wasn't worth putting myself out there all the time.

So when I had moved to Los Angeles to attend graduate school at the University of Southern California, I decided to take a more passive approach to dating. I was going to concentrate on becoming as cool as I possibly could. And then I would just let the girls come to me. That was my plan, at least. If I had learned anything from Lilly, it was that you can't force something that isn't there. A girl either likes you or she doesn't. So now I was taking the Whole Foods approach to finding a girlfriend: I was going to let it happen organically.

Most of my friends from college were living in Washington, DC, now, but I was out in gloriously sunny but lonely Los Angeles pursuing a master's degree in communications. I was living in a ten-by-ten-foot dorm room on campus at USC, a room about the size of a walk-in closet. There was a cafeteria connected to my dorm where I ate all my meals at a table by myself. As I walked across the palm-tree-decorated campus to class each day, I watched the pretty girls pass me on the sidewalk without ever trying to talk to any of them. If they were interested, they would talk to me, I figured.

But at the moment I met Sasha, I happened to be in North Dakota, which is kind of the opposite of Los Angeles: no beaches, no warm sun, no overcrowding. There aren't as many beautiful people as in LA, either, which is what made this girl with the crown stand out even more.

"Official business, huh?" I said. "Are you, like, queen of an obscure nation where they speak English with American accents?"

"Yes. It's called North Dakota. And actually if you listen carefully, we have our own accent up here."

"You're Miss North Dakota," I said, realizing who she was.

"And you're Josh. Nice to meet you. I'm Sasha."

She held out her hand and I shook it.

"How did you—"

"I saw you speak earlier," she interrupted. "Nice presentation. You're very funny."

"Full disclosure—I'm not as funny in real life."

"Well, I don't see any other guys my age talking to me right now, so I'll just have to settle for an unamusing conversation with you."

It was true: There weren't any other boys her age talking to her or, for that matter, in this entire hotel ballroom. We were at a middle school leadership conference. My motivational speaking career had started to take off while I was in grad school, and I was at the conference as the keynote speaker. I had started giving speeches while I was in high school, and by the time I was ski racing I was getting paid for it. So during my years as a ski racer, I gave a few speeches a year to fund my training. Anyway, now that I was in grad school I was thinking I might want to make speaking my full-time profession. Especially if the job gave me the chance to meet girls like Sasha.

She had presented a workshop on bullying, according to what I'd read in the program. This was the final night of the conference, and the five hundred middle school attendees were grinding merrily on one another on the dance floor in the center of the room. Sasha and I were planted firmly against the wall, watching the spectacle from a safe distance and speaking loudly enough that we could hear each other over the music.

"So how come you aren't dancing?" I asked.

"I could ask you the same question."

"They're all minors. I'm not trying to end up in one of your North Dakota jails."

She was tall, blond, and 100 percent bombshell. The regally formal tiara on her head was mismatched with the casual chic of her outfit: a light blue baby-doll T-shirt, skinny jeans, and magenta heels.

"Well, the truth is." She leaned her head a little closer to mine and lowered her voice. "I don't dance."

I raised my eyebrows. She continued reluctantly.

"In fact, this is the first real dance I've ever been to."

"You usually attend fake dances?"

"Basically. I was homeschooled," she said.

"Oh, you're one of *those*!"

She frowned. "Yeah, I guess I am."

"I'm kidding! I was homeschooled, too."

She grabbed both my hands and her heels bounced off the floor with excitement. Maybe she could dance better than she thought. "You *were*?"

"Until high school."

"Gee whiz! I was homeschooled till college!"

"That's crazy," I said. "And may I say, I've never heard someone use the term 'gee whiz' if they weren't being sarcastic."

Just then, the song changed.

"Oh, I love this one!" she said.

It was "California Love" by Tupac.

"Fun fact, I live in Los Angeles, and in California we sing this in place of the national anthem."

She looked horrified. "Really?"

"No, not really. You need to get out of your state more."

The first verse began and she started rapping along, word for word, pumping an open palm with the beat.

I said, "I thought you said you don't dance."

"I'm not dancing. I'm rapping."

"What's the difference?"

"Um, seriously? Like, think about it: Tupac doesn't dance. He raps."

"Didn't dance."

"What?"

"*Didn't* dance. Past tense. He's dead."

She laughed. "Oh, you're one of *those*."

"One of whats?"

"Those people who think Tupac is dead. Haven't you read his lyrics? His posthumous albums reference Bill Clinton, who was elected years after Tupac was supposedly murdered, excuse me, assassinated."

"You're the only homeschooler I've ever met who studies Tupac lyrics."

"I bet I'm also the only homeschooler you've ever met who's a Miss America contestant. Perhaps you noticed the crown?"

"Yes, as a matter of fact."

"It is somewhat conspicuous."

"And very official-business-looking."

She motioned with her head so her tiara pointed toward the back of the room.

"Let's go get some snacks," she suggested.

I followed her. I would've followed her across the border to Canada.

She piled a little snack plate high with food.

"Most pageant girls are always like"—she adjusted her voice to a whiny, nasally pitch—"*OMG, I can't eat any carbs or I'll get fat.*"

I've found that whenever a girl uses the word "fat" in a sentence, it's probably a trick of some sort, and the safest strategy is to say nothing. So I remained silent.

"Anyway," she said, switching back to her normal Sasha voice, "I'm like, screw that, I'm hungry!"

I nodded and said nothing in case this was also a trick.

"So how long are you in North Dakota?" she asked. She did indeed have a slight accent, pronouncing the name of her state like *Noor Dakoewwwwda*.

"Just till tomorrow."

"When do you roll out?"

"Flight leaves at six AM," I said.

She grimaced.

"I know, right? Too early," I said.

"No. Too soon."

The next morning, when I took a taxi to the airport, it was both predawn and subzero, a highly unpleasant intersection of elements that sucks the life directly out of your soul. At the top of the escalator just before airport security, I found Sasha sitting on a bench. She was wearing sweatpants, a hoodie, and thick-framed retro glasses. Her hair was pulled back in a loose ponytail. She was gorgeous.

She stood, smiling.

When you see someone unexpectedly and it is clear that person is there to surprise you, it's tough to conjure the right words. Or for that matter to conjure any words at all. You're just so confused.

"What are you doing here?" I managed to say.

"I came to tell you good-bye."

"It's very early."

"I stayed up all night."

"You do that normally?"

"Only when I want to make sure I'm up very early."

There was a pause.

"So where's the crown?" I asked.

"This isn't official business."

I hoped it wasn't business at all. I hoped it was personal. I mean, it had to be, right? Why else would someone show up at the airport at such a soul-sucking hour?

"So...it's nice to see you again. Also—I don't know—I was thinking I could get your, or maybe..."

"Josh, are you trying to ask for my number?"

"No. Well, yes. I mean, only if you want to give it to me."

She handed me a slip of paper on which her number had already been written.

"Call me."

"I will," I said. "And actually, I'll be back here for another speech in a couple weeks."

"Really?" she asked, her face brightening.

"Yeah," I said. "We should hang out sometime. I mean, then. We should hang out then, at that time."

"I would like that."

"In the meantime, practice those dance moves," I said.

"Maybe I will."

"What's your talent, by the way?"

"You mean for Miss America?"

"Yeah."

"Stripping."

My mouth dropped open slightly.

"I'm kidding."

"Oh."

"I sing opera."

"Opera, huh? I guess that's kind of like stripping."

"Kind of. They both involve funny costumes."

"I wouldn't know. I stay away."

"Too bad. You might like it. Opera, I mean."

"That's the one I stay away from. And the other one, too. But I gotta go catch my flight. I'll talk to you soon."

Chapter 32

— — — — — — — — —

I felt my phone vibrate in my pocket, so I stopped in the middle of the sidewalk and pulled it out. Sasha. It had been a few weeks now since we met, and we talked almost every day.

"Hey!" I said.

"Hey, what are you up to?"

"I was just walking back from class."

"*Was* walking? Why did you stop?"

"I can't walk and hold my phone at the same time. Well, I can, but then I have to use one hand to hold the phone and walk with one crutch, and it's pretty difficult, so, you know."

"Oh, right," she said.

I liked that she had to be reminded I had one leg and was on crutches, how that was not the first thing she saw when she imagined me. It was different for the students who were passing me on the sidewalk as I stood there talking on my phone. All they saw was the missing leg. They would take quick glances and then look away, torn between the universal instinct to examine that which is different and the learned social behavior that it's rude to stare.

Sasha's voice on the phone interrupted my thoughts. "If you don't mind my asking, how come you don't wear your prosthesis anymore? In your speech you talked about it, but I never saw you wearing it."

"Oh, I have nerve problems. Vestigial pain from my amputation. The leg is really uncomfortable. I can't wear it anymore."

"You can't, I don't know, fix it?"

"No, I went to a bunch of doctors. The only thing they can do is a nerve-blocking surgery on my spinal cord."

"Eek."

"That's what I said. I get around fine on my crutches, so it's not a big deal. In some ways it's better—socially, I mean."

"How's that?" she asked. I usually didn't talk much about my amputation when I was getting to know a girl. I would prefer not to emphasize it. But I know people are always curious, Sasha included, and now I'd given her a window of opportunity to ask questions.

"Well, it's like, before, when I used to wear my leg," I explained, gesticulating now with my free hand, balancing on one leg, crutches hanging off my forearms, "people saw me limping on what they didn't know was a prosthesis and they were always curious what was wrong with me. They would say stuff like, 'Did you sprain your ankle?' and I had to be like, 'Um, no, my leg was amputated.'"

"Awkward." She laughed.

"Exactly. So now it's really obvious — like right now everyone on the sidewalk where I'm standing can see that I have one leg. But at least there's no question about what sort of disability I have. I'm not trying to disguise it with a fake leg or something. It's like, what you see is what you get."

"Yeah. That makes sense. That's cool. But don't people treat you differently because you have one leg?"

"Of course. All the time. I get asked the weirdest questions."

"That's how I feel being, you know, a pageant girl. Whenever I show up at an event with my tiara and the sash on, I can tell people have certain ideas about me."

"Like what?"

"That I'm pretty, so I must be really dumb. That I'm blond, so I must be an airhead. That I want world peace, but don't really know what world peace is. All that stuff."

"I feel like you can use that to your advantage."

"How do you mean?" she asked.

"Like, people make assumptions about me because I have one leg, right? When they meet me, I mean. They figure that I'm probably very shy, reserved, self-conscious.

That I might be bitter about my situation. So, it's like, if I act really confident and self-assured, it bowls people over. It's shocking. They are amazed by my charisma or something, but it's only because their expectations were so low in the first place. I feel like you can have the same effect."

"Aww, you're saying you think I'm smarter than the average beauty queen?"

"Now you're just fishing for compliments."

That semester I also started traveling to North Dakota pretty often for speeches. I always thought about Kyle and his steel-toed boot, how I needed to bite the bullet and have a DTR with Sasha, tell her I liked her. For one thing, maybe she'd win Miss America. And if she did, I needed to make sure I was dating her before then, because once she had that national crown she'd be way, way out of my league.

But more importantly, we needed to have the talk for the reason you always need to have the talk: so things can

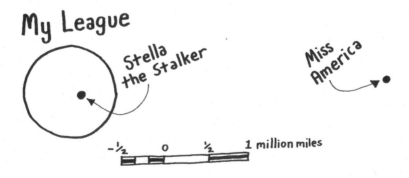

My League

Stella the Stalker

Miss America

-½   0   ½   1 million miles

move forward, so you can emerge from the muck of ambiguity into a mutually understood, solidified relationship.

That's where the long-distance thing was a real impediment, though, because you really don't want to have a DTR over the phone. That's a conversation you must have face-to-face. But during those brief hours when we'd be together in North Dakota, in between my speeches and her public appearances, the time was just so short. I couldn't bring myself to do it. It was like high school all over again.

What I needed was a grand romantic gesture, a big display, a smash-bang, knock-her-socks-off surprise that would either cause us to implode or to become boyfriend and girlfriend. Like a rooftop picnic. Like a canoeing date on a lake. Like a national beauty pageant.

Chapter 33

— — — — — — — — —

I was pretty sure Sasha was going to win Miss America. I just had a feeling. And I was also pretty sure she liked me. I had a feeling about that, too. My idea was to bring these two feelings together in my grand gesture. Specifically, I would show up to surprise her at the pageant. Like when she surprised me at the airport. Except after sunrise.

In fact, it would not be enough for me to be merely in the audience at the pageant, just one of seven thousand anonymous faces. I needed access to her before she got onstage. But how?

In the weeks leading up to the pageant, I didn't get to talk with her much on the phone. She was spending all her time getting pedicures, manicures, and all the other types of cures available from the cosmetology industry. You would think she was a tribute in the Hunger Games or something. Not that she needed it; she was beautiful before. But Miss America has to be perfect.

Meanwhile, after a great deal of planning and effort, I found my back door into the pageant. I made an arrangement with an organization that was one of the sponsors of Miss America. I would give a motivational speech at an event for this group. In exchange, they would get me a ticket to the pageant in Las Vegas. Not only that, they would also get me a ticket to a super-ballin', VIP, two-thousand-dollar-a-plate banquet the night before. A banquet, it should be noted, where all the pageant contestants would be in attendance.

So I road-tripped across the desert from Los Angeles to Las Vegas, fantasizing the whole way about the look on Sasha's face when she saw me at this banquet, decked out in the tuxedo I had purchased on eBay just for the occasion. She would be overcome by the pageantry of my grand gesture, by the affection and loyalty and sacrifice it all signaled. I mean, who could resist a boyfriend who would do all that for you?

I wore my tuxedo on the drive to Las Vegas, all its parts with the exception of the final piece of the outfit: the bow tie. Let me back up and explain that I had decided to wear a *real* bow tie at this event, not the pre-tied, clip-on variety I wore when I took Evelyn to prom. Before departing for my drive, I had studied several bow tie tutorials online and planned to put it on once I arrived at the casino.

I walked into Planet Hollywood, the location of both

the banquet and the pageant, on my crutches with my bow tie in my pocket. I was nervous; I could run into Sasha at any point now, I figured. And I really wanted our meeting to be perfect. I wanted to take her breath away. I wanted her to be so happy I had come to see her. I wanted her to say, *Gee whiz, you came all this way to cheer for me at the pageant? Holy smokes! Can I be your girlfriend, please?*

I ducked into a men's room outside the ballroom where the banquet would be held. Standing in front of the mirror, I extracted the bow tie from my pocket and attempted to replicate the steps I had studied in those tutorials. But no luck. I quickly discovered that real bow ties, while they look very classy, very James Bond–like, are virtually impossible to tie. Or at least, to tie perfectly. With every attempt I made, it always ended up crooked or lopsided, or tilted at a forty-five-degree angle. I was getting frustrated. And sweaty. And worried. I was worried that this was taking too long and I was going to miss the whole banquet. I was going to miss Sasha. I was going to miss my chance with her. Or I would see her, but my bow tie would make me look like a clown, and she would be all like, *Um, no, you aren't quite classy enough for me, Mr. Lopsided Bow Tie.*

The real bow tie had seemed like such a cool idea. I had expected it would make me look so suave and sophisticated. Now I saw that it was a mistake—a big, fat, carb-bloated mistake. It just wasn't worth it. I had spent too much time trying to get it to look right and it had not even been close to worth it. Next time I wore a tuxedo, I decided, I would revert to prom-style clip-on bow ties. They were oh-so-much easier to put on.

About this time one of the other banquet attendees walked in. He was also clad in a tuxedo, but his bow tie was already tied. I was jealous of its symmetry.

I'm not sure what it is about having one leg that makes people want to comment on it. But for some reason my disability gives many individuals permission in their own minds to say whatever they want despite our being total strangers. And often what they say ends up being quite awkward. Especially the questions they ask.

I'll give you an example. One time I was wearing my artificial leg, and I was talking to this girl about what it was made out of, how it worked, all that. She looked down at the prosthesis, and she was like, "Is the foot fake, too?"

I informed her about the amazing medical technology that had allowed doctors to attach my real foot to the end of my artificial leg.

"Really?" she said.

Let me clarify: This wasn't a child. This girl was in high school.

So anyway, I was standing in the men's room getting very frustrated about how the real bow tie had not been worth all the trouble, and this gentleman walked in, and he said to me, "It looks like you do pretty well with that."

Now, reader, I was currently so caught up in my bow-tying experience that I assumed he was talking about *my ability to tie a real bow tie,* though he was in fact talking about my ability to navigate life with one leg. So I was like, "Well, thanks. I appreciate that."

A few seconds later this gentleman and I were both standing in front of the urinals. I want to remind you that I was thinking about my bow tie, about how the real bow tie just wasn't worth the trouble. And he was thinking about my life as an amputee.

I said, staring at the wall above the urinal, "I tell you though, it's actually pretty difficult."

I could see him nodding out of the corner of my eye. "Yeah, it looks like it would be . . . pretty difficult."

There was a pause. "To be honest," I confessed, "tonight I've been feeling like it's just not even worth it anymore."

He blatantly broke the number one rule of social interaction at urinals, making direct eye contact with me, and exclaimed, "Son, it's always worth it! No matter what happens—it's always worth it!"

This guy is intense, I thought. I must look really good in a real bow tie after all.[11] Maybe even good enough to impress Sasha?

At the banquet, I was seated at a circular table with a bunch of people I didn't know. This wasn't particularly surprising, of course, since I didn't really know anyone at

---

[11] It wasn't until a few weeks later that I was thinking about how strange that conversation was, and it dawned on me what a massive misunderstanding we'd had. That guy is probably still out there organizing candlelit prayer vigils for me.

the event. I made small talk with my table-neighbors, however, all the while waiting and watching for the pageant contestants to arrive.

And arrive they did. As dessert was being served, the lights went down in the small ballroom. Conversation among the crowd quieted down. A tuxedoed guy with well-coiffed gray hair took the podium. He looked like a boxing promoter—like the "Let's get ready to rumble" guy. In fact, he probably *was* the "Let's get ready to rumble" guy. This was Vegas, after all. He asked us to please put our hands together for this year's *Miss Aaaaaaaaaamerica contestaaaants,* and we did as instructed. Spotlights came on as the fifty-two girls[12] marched into the room wearing evening gowns and sashes embroidered with the names of their home states. As it happened, Miss North Dakota walked right by my table. We made brief eye contact, and then her head snapped back when she recognized me. She stepped out of the line and let the other girls keep walking as she approached my table.

I stood up and reached out for a hug that never quite materialized.

All she said was, "I didn't know you were going to be here."

There was no excitement in her voice, no gratitude, no happiness. She wasn't even smiling.

---

[12] In answer to your question: DC and Puerto Rico.

This was not how I had imagined it. Not what I had planned. Not at all. I felt like I was falling, like I had lost my balance and was dropping in slow motion to land hard on the grass beside a golf tee.

"I—I wanted it to be a surprise," I said eventually.

She blinked a few times like a flashbulb had gone off unexpectedly in front of her. She looked surprised, all right, but not in a good way.

"Oh, okay, well—I have to go sit at my table."

And then her tiara rose several inches as she returned to perfect posture and fell back into the procession of beauty queens, left hand planted on her hip, right hand sashaying with each step.

I didn't see her again that night. I hoped she would at least text me, but she never did. I got a cheap room at a Motel 6 off the main Strip that had a single lonely slot machine in the lobby. At the pageant the next day, I sat by myself and cheered extra loud for Sasha. Out of the fifty-two contestants, she was one of only two who wore a one-piece bathing suit instead of a bikini. Sasha was a homeschooler, I remembered, and though she did listen to gangsta rap, I supposed at heart she was still a good Christian girl. So she stuck to her guns and kept things modest onstage. I had to respect her principled stand, though a part of me wished she would've sold out a little, showed off a little more skin. Not for me. For the judges. For the win.

Because she didn't win. In fact, she didn't even make

the top fifteen, so I never got to hear her sing opera. Oh well. I wouldn't have understood the words anyway.

After the pageant ended, I walked around Vegas for a couple of hours, hoping she would text or call to see if we could hang out, or at least to thank me for coming. I walked up and down the entire length of the Strip. I stepped inside a few of the casinos and watched retirees blowing their savings one slot machine pull at a time. I waved away hobo-looking dudes offering glossy postcards with scantily clad women. I stared silently for a really long time at the fountain in front of the Bellagio. But I never heard from Sasha. Not once. Nothing. So I drove back through the desert to Los Angeles feeling angry, hurt, confused.

How could I have been so inaccurate in my assessment of our relationship? I mean, I wasn't in high school anymore. I felt like my instincts had matured enough that I could usually tell when a girl liked me. And Sasha had always seemed interested. Really interested. She had come to see me at the airport when it was still dark outside. We'd talked on the phone constantly ever since. We'd hung out in North Dakota whenever I came to town and always, it had seemed, had a great time. Granted, we had never kissed, but our hugs had been lingering and, honestly, I thought we were practically boyfriend and girlfriend. Yet, when I came to surprise and support her on the most important day of her life, she hardly even noticed I was there. Not before the pageant, not after.

I gave it a few more days. Maybe she was busy. Maybe she was bummed about her loss. Maybe she had a bunch of formal gowns to pack up and ship home. Maybe she'd call me when she got back to North Dakota.

Nope. I never heard anything from her. So I didn't call her, either. I didn't text. But as the days turned into weeks and my final semester at USC finished up, I kept wondering: What happened? Where had I gone wrong? How had I misjudged our relationship so drastically?

HYPOTHESIS

Subject behavior at Miss America pageant suggests I misjudged her interest in me. But if she did not have interest in dating me, why did she spend so much time on the phone with me?

Face-to-face interview is required to investigate.

INVESTIGATION

Chapter 34

— — — — — — — — —

A few months after the Christmas when I tracked down the girls of my failed middle school and high school relationships, I happened to be in Sasha's home state of North Dakota for a speech. In fact, I was in her city. Her number was still in my phone, so I broke radio silence by sending her a text to ask if she wanted to have dinner while I was in town.

And that's how I found myself at a booth with Sasha in a sushi place that had a little fountain in the middle of it. I was nervous. Our conversation was basically an act of verbal procrastination.

Eventually, she asked, "So, you have a girlfriend?"

"No. Do you have a boyfriend?"

She shook her head, smiling like that was a funny question. "No. No boyfriend."

"Speaking of which..."

She raised her eyebrows.

I continued, "Remember when we were—I mean,

remember when we used to be—remember..." This was not going well so far. "When I came to Las Vegas? To the Miss America pageant?"

"Of course."

"That was a big deal for me."

"I bet. That banquet was two thousand dollars a plate."

I smiled. "Oh yeah. I got a free ticket."

"How?"

"This whole time you thought I paid two grand for it?"

"How'd you get it?"

"Doesn't matter now. Look, what I want to know is, how come you blew me off that night?"

"What?"

"You blew me off. You barely said a word to me."

"Josh, I was about to compete in *Miss America*."

"And I had just paid two thousand dollars to see you do it."

"I thought your ticket was free."

"It was. But you didn't know that."

"The pageant was the biggest day of my life. It was a whirlwind. I barely even talked to my parents."

Our waitress arrived with my seaweed salad.

"So how come you never called me afterward?"

"After what?"

"The pageant."

She frowned. "You mean after I lost?"

"After you competed in Miss America."

"I was eliminated in the first round."

"So? You were one of the top fifty-two girls *in the country*. In America!"

"Josh, what did you place in the Paralympics?"

"Thirty-fourth."

"And were you proud of that finish?"

I was silent.

"Were you?"

"I see your point."

"Answer the question, please."

"No, I thought it was a pretty bad finish."

"But Josh! You were at the Paralympics! You were one of the top ski racers... *in the world*!"

"All right, all right, I understand."

"Do you? I don't think you do. Because that's why I didn't call you, if you must know. You had paid all that money and traveled all that way to see me compete. I wanted you to see me win and wanted you to be my boyfriend. But I lost. And I was ashamed about that. I was embarrassed."

It was a lot to process. But above everything she had just said, blinking like a neon sign in Vegas, was a single word: "boyfriend."

"You liked me?" I asked.

"Of course I liked you."

"So why didn't you call me?"

"I could ask you the same question."

"I didn't call you because you blew me off. I thought you had started dating someone else or something."

"Well, you were wrong."

But then it occurred to me: We could make things right. Now that it was all out in the open, now that we were both single and sitting there together in this sushi restaurant...

"Maybe it's not too late," I said.

"No, it is."

"But why? Just because we live far apart?"

"Josh—"

"We could come visit each other."

"Josh—"

"Sasha, we could make this work!"

"*Josh!*"

"What?"

She looked down at the table silently.

"What?" I said again.

She kept her gaze fixed. I followed it down to her hand, where I noticed for the first time a sparkling diamond ring. I blinked a few times.

"I thought you said you don't have a boyfriend," I said softly.

"I don't. I have a fiancé."

"Oh. Well. Congratulations," I said unconvincingly. "When did you meet?"

"Three months ago. We got engaged six weeks later."

I didn't say anything, but I guess my surprise was written all over my face.

"When you know, you know," she said. "You just have to find the right person."

"I wouldn't know."

RESULTS OF
INVESTIGATION

Chapter 35

— — — — — — — — —

I went back to my hotel room and lay on the bed and stared at the ceiling. Sasha was the final girl on my list, so the scientific investigation was now complete. Complete, but not insightful. I had no answer, no single unifying explanation as to why I could never find a girlfriend. I had found no fatal flaw in my personality or appearance like I had expected to. The investigation, I concluded, had been a complete failure.

Some months went by. One night I went to see a movie by myself. Near the end, one of the characters lost a limb. Which happens in movies all the time, right? No big deal. The lights came up and I walked out to my car and sat down in the driver's seat. Then I started to breathe all weird. Oxygen came in short gasps. I thought about the character in that movie, and then I was thinking about the little boy I had once been, the boy who had lost a limb of his own, and I felt incredibly sorry for him. I wished I could reach back through time and hold his hand, comfort him in some way. I felt such grief over his life. Over my life.

A little gasp came out of my mouth, and then I was crying.

I thought, why am I crying? This doesn't make sense. My amputation was so long ago. I am over it. I have accepted it and moved on with my life. Right?

And that's when I realized the real reason, the actual reason, I had set out on my scientific investigation in the first place: I wanted to find an explanation, any explanation at all, other than the obvious one. I had always been the guy who had *overcome* his amputation. I mean, I went to the Paralympics. I had been an elite athlete, a world-ranked ski racer. I had never used my disability as an excuse for anything. That just wasn't the kind of person I was. So I had not wanted to blame it for my lack of success with girls, either.

And if I was honest with myself, this was why I had really begun the investigation. I had hoped the girls I interviewed would tell me that I had been too nerdy, or too serious, or too silly, or too anything, really. In fact, I would have even considered my investigation successful if one or two of the girls had told me they didn't want to date me because I was an amputee. At least that would allow me to say to myself: See, there is a problem, and the problem is with these girls being too shallow to date a guy with a disability. In other words, the problem is with them and their psychological shortcomings, not with me and mine.

But of course, no girls had told me that. The truth was, *I* was the one who had a problem with my disability. Sitting there in the parking lot crying, I finally admitted to myself that I was deeply and painfully insecure about it. That was why I never tried to talk to Liza Taylor after the pumpkin shoe–relay incident. That was why I was too scared to kiss Francesca at the waterfall. That was why I had never told Evelyn my true feelings about her. And that was why I had lost my nerve with Sasha and stopped calling her after the pageant. Because I was insecure about having one leg. It made me doubt myself. It made me feel inferior. I had always known this, deep down, but I had not wanted to admit that there was an element of my disability I had yet to overcome, so I concocted this investigation to find some other explanation on which to place blame.

And for this reason, my hypotheses had all been flawed from the beginning. The problem had not been with the girls, and the problem had not been with some characteristic of mine; the problem had been with my believing there was a problem. It had been with my believing that the way my body was shaped disqualified me from having a romantic relationship. It was not the shape of my body, as it turned out, but my insecurities about that shape that had kept me single.

ASHLEY
SAMSONITE

Eleven Months Later

— — ~ — — — — — —

It was Saturday night and I was out with my college friends. My brother Matt was also in town, visiting his girlfriend, who lived here in DC. We were dancing it up at a place called Local 16, a relatively classy restaurant located in a historic three-story row house on U Street. At night, they cleared away the tables upstairs, brought in a DJ, and lowered the lights, and the space turned into a small, sweaty, kinetic dance floor.

After a while of dancing/jumping/flailing with my crew, this girl came up to me and asked about my tie. I wear ties for this exact purpose. Not to try to look good, but because they can be a good conversation starter. They give girls an excuse to talk to you. So we were standing there talking about my tie and whatnot, and this girl with platinum-blond hair and a silver spaghetti-strap dress walks up to me from the other direction and says, "You're awesome."

Girl Number Two was drop-dead gorgeous, absolutely

stunning. And she just walked up to initiate a conversation—*with me!* How often does that happen? Um, like, never. This was a once-in-a-lifetime kind of opportunity. But being the gentleman that I am, I felt I owed chronological preference to Girl Number One. I couldn't just blow her off and start talking to the blonde simply because I preferred the way she looked. That's not how my mother raised me, you know?

So I gave a terse thanks over my shoulder to Girl Number Two and then turned my back on her to continue discussing the fascinating history of my tie with Girl Number One. Girl Number Two walked away, disappearing from my life for what I assumed would be forever.

Eventually I broke free of the conversation with Girl Number One (who, as it turned out, had a boyfriend—*so why was she even asking about my tie in the first place?*) and returned to dancing with my crew. I told them the story, yelling over the music. Girl Number Two. The hot blonde. A sad missed opportunity. Just my luck.

After a few songs, I noticed that not three feet in front of me was the back of a blond head. I turned to Matt.

"Hey, isn't that the girl who said I was awesome earlier?"

Matt agreed that *Yeah, dude, it was totally her.*

The problem was that now there was a guy hitting on her. And as soon as she shut him down and sent him walking away with his head hanging, another guy jumped in to fill his place.

I knew she already thought I was awesome. The door was open for me to talk to her. The problem was the continuous stream of bros trying to hit on her. And then there was this moment when she was gloriously alone, just standing there dancing by herself. I reached out to tap her on the shoulder, but reflexively pulled my hand back before it touched her. I had just witnessed this girl shutting down five guys in a row! Who cared if she thought I was awesome? She was clearly in the zone — the rejection zone — demolishing egos with ruthless efficiency.

No, this was no time to back down. I'd come too far. I'd learned too much. About girls. About myself. I wouldn't miss this one.

I tapped her on the shoulder. She turned around, eyebrows raised.

"Aren't you the girl who said I was awesome earlier?"

"Yeah, I am," she said, smiling.

I felt a warm tingle all over my body. She was clearly happy to be talking to me again. Now all I had to do was chat with her for a few minutes, dance with her for a while, and she would offer me her number at the end of the night and this would be the beginning of —

"We're leaving."

The voice came from another girl, a tall brunette, whose tone communicated *My ex-boyfriend showed up here* or *I just saw another girl wearing the same dress as me* or some other such female night-ruining disaster.

"Oh . . . all right," said the blonde.

"Wait, you're leaving *right now*?" I asked.

"Yeah," she said. "Sorry."

She did look genuinely sorry, but she was being pulled on the wrist by the girl who was not having fun. She got dragged a few steps away and started to disappear into the crowd.

"Wait!" I called. "What's your name? I'll Facebook you."

Notice: not a yes-or-no question. So she couldn't reject it.

She smiled. "Ashley Samsonite."

"All right. Got it. I'll friend you, okay?"

She nodded and then she was gone.

I turned to Brad.

"You remember Ashley. I'll remember Samsonite."

His forehead wrinkled. "What?"

"Ashley. Just remember that name, all right?"

"Ashley. Got it."

I spent the rest of the evening repeating her last name over and over in my mind so I wouldn't forget it. It was my only connection to her, the sole thread holding us together. Samsonite, Samsonite, Samsonite.

When Brad and I got back to our apartment, I immediately logged in to Facebook, assuming there couldn't be more than a few Ashley Samsonites out there. Wrong. There were over six hundred of them. The search results showed their profile pictures as unrecognizably tiny thumbnails. Plus, because of privacy settings, I couldn't see where most of them lived, so I was not able to simply sort by who resided in DC. I spent the next two hours scrolling through the search results and friending every single Ashley Samsonite who was blond and either lived in DC or did not specify a hometown. It was three AM when I reached the end of the list, having friended around thirty girls with identical names. I had waited too long to meet this girl. I was not going to lose her now.

When I woke up the next morning, I signed in to Facebook and found that five Ashley Samsonites had accepted my friend request. Five! This made me wonder: Assuming that one of them was the "real" Ashley Samsonite, who were these other four girls? They get a friend request from some random guy with one leg and say, *Sure, I'll be friends with him?*

Also, when the real Ashley saw my friend request and looked at my profile, presumably she saw on my timeline an activity feed something like this:

Josh Sundquist is now friends with Ashley Samsonite
Josh Sundquist is now friends with Ashley Samsonite
Josh Sundquist is now friends with Ashley Samsonite
Awkward.

Anyway, I checked out the five Ashley Samsonites who had accepted my friendship. Now that I was friends with them, and could see their photos in full size, I was able to pick out the one I had met the previous night. So I sent her a message about how we should, you know, hang out sometime.

One night a few months and many perfect dates later, she agreed to let me be her boyfriend.

And just like that, I had a girlfriend. I looked at myself later that night in the mirror and noticed, somewhat to my

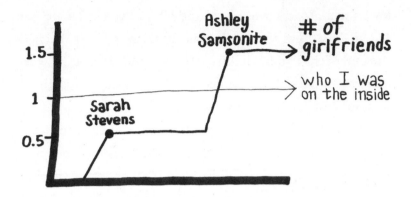

surprise, that I looked pretty much the same as I did before. I was still the same person I had been all along, the person I'd always been inside, the one who was always worthy of a relationship, always worthy of love. Being an amputee doesn't make me a fraction of a person. The whole is greater than the sum of its parts. I am whole just the way I am.

A few weeks later Ashley and I were out dancing, and I started to lose my balance. Normally, when this happens, I put out a crutch to steady myself. Or, if I'm not fast enough with the crutch, I fall. But on this night of dancing with my girlfriend, before either of those things could happen, Ashley caught me and pulled me back to center. I stopped dancing and looked at her.

"What?" she asked.

"No one has ever done that for me before," I said.

And that's what I love about Ashley. She keeps me balanced. And she just won't let me fall.

ACKNOWLEDGMENTS

Thanks to Miss America 2010 for (sarcastically) suggesting the idea for this book. (To watch a video about that awkward encounter, Google my name and "Miss America Made Fun of Me.")

Thanks to my agent, Lucy Carson, for (not sarcastically) suggesting that the time was right to put this story on paper. Gratitude to the rest of the Friedrich Agency for their support of my writing, including Nichole LeFebvre and Molly Friedrich.

Most of the good parts of this project, including the graphs, the subtitle, and the organizational format, were suggestions by a wonderful human being without whom the book itself would not exist. I'm speaking of my brilliant editor, Elizabeth Bewley.

Many wonderful suggestions also came from Elizabeth's team, Pam Garfinkel and Pam Gruber. Thanks, Pams.

I am grateful to Little, Brown Books for Young Readers for getting behind this project, especially my publicist, Hallie Patterson; my marketer, Jennifer LaBracio; and director of publicity Melanie Chang. Appreciation to my sales team, Shawn Foster and Dave Epstein.

For the last several years, I've been incredibly lucky to have a smart and talented assistant, Lisa McLaughlin, who works tirelessly behind the scenes to hold the Sundquist Company LLC together. Thanks, Lisa.

Thanks to the girls I've described in this book for their kind and generous conversations, which helped me come to a better understanding of myself and my life. I want to acknowledge that the girl I've called Francesca ended up writing me a long and thoughtful message about our relationship, but unfortunately I received it after the text of this book was already finalized.

Shout-out to my YouTube subscribers for being the first audience to hear many of these stories as they were happening in my life. I'm particularly grateful to those who helped me get started on YouTube, especially iJustine and the Vlog-Brothers (a.k.a. Hank and John Green).

Thanks most of all to my family and friends for making life worthwhile, and for tolerating me writing about them in (yet another) book.